T0115118

INTERVENTION:
REDUCING COMPASSION FATIGUE

About to give up on someone who needs help?

Al Jameson,
Licensed Professional Counselor,
Licensed Chemical Dependency Counselor

WESTBOW
PRESS
A DIVISION OF THOMAS NELSON

ISBN: 978-1-4497-5952-0 (sc)
ISBN: 978-1-4497-5953-7 (e)
ISBN: 978-1-4497-5954-4 (hc)

Library of Congress Control Number: 2012912567

WestBow Press books may be ordered through booksellers or by contacting:

WestBow Press
A Division of Thomas Nelson
1663 Liberty Drive
Bloomington, IN 47403
www.westbowpress.com
1-(866) 928-1240

Quotations designated (NIV) are from THE HOLY BIBLE: NEW INTERNATIONAL VERSION®. NIV®. Copyright © 1973, 1978, 1984 by Biblica. All rights reserved worldwide.

Quotations designated (NIRV) are from the Holy Bible, New International Reader's Version® Copyright © 1995, 1996, 1998 by Biblica. All rights reserved worldwide.

Printed in the United States of America

WestBow Press rev. date: 07/17/2012

INTERVENTION

REDUCES

COMPASSION

FATIGUE

A PRACTICAL, STEP-BY-STEP GUIDE
DISCUSSING THE DANCE OR PROCESS
OF ASKING A TROUBLED
ACQUAINTANCE
TO ACCEPT DIRELY NEEDED
ASSISTANCE.

NEED HELP TO CONFRONT?

CONFRONTATION IS YOUR FRIEND
AND
IS THE FRIEND OF THE ONE YOU LOVE!

SERENITY IS NOT THE ABSENCE OF
CONFRONTATION!
SERENITY IS DEALING WITH
CONFRONTATION
EFFECTIVELY, WITHOUT COMPASSION FATIGUE,
EFFICIENTLY AND RESPECTFULLY.

SERENITY IS THE OPPOSITE OF
COMPULSIVITY.

Contents

INTRODUCTION

Dear Reader,

This book is designed to help religious leaders, professional counselors, concerned family members, and individuals offer viable appropriate levels of care to someone with an addiction problem or a person who refuses to accept assisted living conditions or comply with medical advice. Use the tools in this book to increase the awareness of the issue and acceptance of recovery.

Learn how to avoid compassion fatigue while using healthy personal boundaries. Because these tools are likely used in an emotional setting, the least emotionally involved helper or leader is the best person for attempting an organized intervention. When that less emotionally involved person is not available, a family member may choose to use this material and know they have attempted to offer choices. The family members will be able to find serenity after going through this process.

This book teaches a mini-intervention or one-on-one short meeting as a setup for a full-blown maxi-intervention later, if necessary. If the maxi-intervention is not successful at first, next steps and consequences are taught. These steps are in keeping with Jesus' instructions on how to approach someone with an issue.

This book compiles thirty-nine years of studying and experience of achieving compliance with the best of care for someone refusing help with a serious issue. I have led over 800 family interventions. In using these steps and illustrations, 90 percent of the full maxi-interventions result in beginning the first stages of treatment or recovery. If you or I learn of a more effective approach to a reluctant person with a problem, please let us share. This is simply where I am today on the journey of learning and serving.

Al Jameson, LPC, LCDC

Chapter 1

Do We Need to Confront?

Do you want to help someone with a serious problem who does not want help? He/she either does not realize there is any problem or is refusing to seek viable, available appropriate solutions.

Rather than using "he/she" or "your loved one," allow me to simply refer to them as "Addie" and "he." I will say "problem" to refer to gambling, workaholic concerns, sexual issues, video game obsession, or other damaging excesses. Addie could be a loved one with a religious cult control conflict, or he may have a problem with chemical abuse, including alcohol or any other mind-altering substance, addictions, mental disorder, or noncompliance with medication or medical advice. An intervention also works for an elderly person who refuses to accept a higher level of healthcare, such as assisted living, not taking necessary medication, declining medical attention, or any other perceived problem.

I've helped church leaders gather groups to confront a church member with a spiritual issue, such as compulsive lying or writing hate mail. This is the third step of Jesus' instructions in Matthew 18 to retrieve someone with a problem. Even in a secular setting, I insist on knowing when the prospect needing help was approached one-on-one before I participate in a group confrontation or intervention.

You may be the only one thinking this is a problem. You and/ or others may have tried to approach this person to no avail. If you absolutely cannot engage others to join in an intervention, then this is not the correct approach. I will suggest other approaches later. Addie probably assumed a position to resist all changes. This background can affect all relationships: professional, church, and personal. This material will help you decide if a confrontation is needed and to adopt a better strategy in the myriad dances, processes, or negotiations that happen in the days before and after an intervention. This is really an issue of conflict resolution.

Why Consider an Intervention as Respect and Concern for the One You Love?

- Are you afraid to approach a loved one?

- Intervention is the most effective way to reach many with serious issues.

- Intervention reveals that you care.

- Intervention presents viable, available, appropriate choices in an acceptable way.

- Intervention helps you to stick with healthy boundaries and limit compassion fatigue.

- This assists concerned friends, acquaintances, and families to stop enabling others with harmful behaviors.

- These pages can support professionals in reviewing the steps to assist a family in conducting an intervention.

- Reviewing an intervention will give confidence to families or others concerned with confronting a loved one with a problem or seeking professional assistance to confront the loved one.

- I want to encourage folks who are reluctant to confront or to butt in to another's life. This reluctance to intervene may come from religious or family-of-origin rules. This book offers reasons to consider intervening as an act of love and with expectation of good outcomes.

Common Core Issues from Concerned Others and Addie

- Feeling a lack of approval
- Feeling rejected / not wanted
- Feeling unfairly criticized
- Fear of abandonment
- Fearful of trusting others
- Feeling taken advantage of
- Feeling not listened to
- Feeling unloved
- Feeling put down
- Feeling unimportant
- Feeling smothered
- Feeling helpless
- Feeling not good enough

SELF-TEST: Use the following questions to determine if you are enabling or participating in an out-of-control person's death or if you desire to look into an intervention.

TEST YOURSELF	YES	NO
I have a hard time saying no to others.	( )	( )
I have boundary issues.	( )	( )
I feel angry, hurt, provoked.	( )	( )
I wish they could hear my concern.	( )	( )
I know others are worried or concerned.	( )	( )
I am ready to seek help.	( )	( )
I want to stop participating in any form of abuse: verbal, mental, financial, physical, chemical, spiritual, or self.	( )	( )
I feel guilty for allowing a problem to continue.	( )	( )
I give many "second chances."	( )	( )
I could learn more about enabling, codependency, and caretaking.	( )	( )
I am preparing to take intelligent action.	( )	( )
I am a good, lovable person.	( )	( )
I have an unconditional positive regard for the future of the one needing help.	( )	( )
They do have choices.	( )	( )
They have total responsibility for their choices.	( )	( )

I try too hard to fix, rescue, caretake,
and cover for others. ( ) ( )

I feel used when I try to help. ( ) ( )

After considering this test, do you want to
learn more about how an intervention works? ( ) ( )

Chapter 2

Are You the Best One to Confront?

Most family groups ask me, "Don't you feel guilty encouraging us to talk behind his back? I feel like we are gossiping, meddling, ganging up, and conspiring against our loved one. This does *not* feel like decent activity for a moral family."

Often a group member will say, "You see, we are Christians, and doing this does not seem Christian." This is a common, expected feeling. I felt the same the first time I was invited to help with a friend's intervention in 1973. I didn't show up at the second meeting, so my friend's family arranged a third practice session and urged me to participate. We finally conducted a successful intervention. I was so surprised that this worked, but I saw the value in confronting loved ones with major issues. I started volunteering two evenings per week to learn and to train other groups to offer interventions beginning in 1973.

I am totally convinced that a loving, caring intervention is a very moral, ethical endeavor to help a person with a serious problem to accept needed assistance. The Good Teacher, Jesus, instructed His followers to approach someone with a problem with a one-on-one strategy. However, he had a backup plan. If one-on-one failed, then take one or two others with you. If this failed, He offered a third attempt by taking the individual to a group. If the individual refused to listen to this group, He spelled out consequences. His apostle Matthew wrote these instructions for intervening in chapter 18 of his New Testament book. Because these directions are inspired by God, they work.

I do not feel one bit guilty in assisting or helping to encourage a caring group to confront the one refusing help for a serious problem. A group is not guilty of wrong in conspiring to make commitments of ultimate consequences if the person chooses to reject viable, appropriate, available help that is offered in a loving, caring, and acceptable way. Good people help reconcile folks with seemingly irreconcilable issues. However, to approach someone without carefully prepared remarks would probably do more harm than good.

Seek an Interventionist or Therapist to Help

In addition to the group seeking a way to intervene, professional partners are needed to help the impaired loved one. This will include selecting an interventionist, if desired, to lead the intervention. Treatment facilities, insurance providers, or other professionals can guide you to find a recommended interventionist to help you with the "dance," or process, of reaching serenity. You will find other approaches and ideas as you seek advice. My thoughts are simply where I am today in finding an organized plan to offer apparent, needed help to someone you care about who declines assistance.

Finding a Treatment Program or Solution for the Problem

Before attempting an intervention, make certain a particular treatment facility is available, will accept Addie with your arranged payment plan, has an opening, and will accept Addie's admission on the day and time you propose to arrive. This often is an in-patient treatment facility. The appropriate level of care might be a daytime partial hospital treatment program. The available program could be his agreeing to attend frequent self-help support groups with or without written verification of attendance and compliance. Some issues are addressed by agreeing to see a professional on a regular basis and complying with treatment or medication protocol. I have helped with several interventions when the goal was to gather in an organized, rehearsed group and convince an impaired person to admit to a care center or nursing center. Some may simply need to give up their car and accept home visits by caregivers. It is a disaster to take a loved one who reluctantly agreed to go with you to a possible helpful program, and then be rejected by the treatment program.

Give the proposed admitting treatment facility Addie's identity information and date of birth, if needed, to confirm insurance coverage. Offer the intervention scripts written in this book to the treatment program if they will accept this information. The counselors there probably will not quote from these family scripts but will have awareness of the seriousness of Addie's circumstances. This knowledge can help the staff to gently break through Addie's resolve and resistance. Some facilities seem not to help with interventions or allow you to send them the written facts regarding their proposed patient. The facility may expect Addie to call, do a phone assessment, and express a desire to come to that treatment facility before they consider an admission. I prefer facilities favorable to interventions and those that will take input from caring loved ones. Of course, facilities cannot discuss or give out information without their patient's written and signed release once they are in the facility's care.

Seek Helpers and Their Input

When the proposed treatment program is ready and as available as possible, to the point of preadmission and finances arranged, next involve acquaintances to seek assistance in bringing about the product of the intervention or serenity. These are concerned people who are actual witnesses of inappropriate behavior. Do not involve those who have only heard about the issue. You need witnesses, not hearsay. A common flawed approach says, "Get over here, we are gathering to make Addie get into treatment." This scares potential participants, and they do not show up to help and may sabotage the intervention.

Recruiting the group to gather to discuss an intervention is vital to success. The concerned organizer makes a beginning offer for help. A call to a colleague at work, neighbors, ex-wives, or to the overly protective sister could make or break the deal.

A good call goes like this: "Do you think someone needs to be concerned about Addie - you know, his health or well-being?" If the answer is "Uh no, he is doing just fine. You don't need to be concerned; don't meddle with him!" then this person quite likely will sabotage the bigger negotiation, or "dance," to get him into treatment and recovery. They will warn him of the pending intervention. The reply then is "Okay, you are probably right. I'm just overly worried, let's forget I even called." Or the person's answer might be "Oh, I'm glad someone called, Addie is late and messing up at work, had slurred speech." In this case, the best reply would be "I'm concerned also. I have someone meeting with me to offer various approaches to Addie. Would you join me in evaluating these suggestions? I value your feedback. Please do not tell Addie of our meeting. If we decide to do nothing, it would only harm our relations with him if he heard that we met to discuss his drinking."

Recruiting and preparation with the group may take hours and can stretch from one day to several months while the appropriate group forms and prepares to confront the loved one who refuses to listen or to accept available options. We hope this process does not take too long while Addie's problem progresses to the pits.

You'll need to make a very brief call to current or ex-colleagues, friends, spouses, close or distant relatives, teachers, neighbors, or anyone who may care enough to help.

You may not be the best person to make these initial calls. Do not let this be about you, but about the impaired person with a problem. This is *not* an occasion to be sensitive or thin skinned regarding your personal issues with anyone in the group. My first college class to train to become a counselor was taught by Vick Shaw. His beginning remarks still ring in my ears. He said, and I cleaned this up some: "You do not have to have all your stuff together to help someone, but you need to get your stuff together enough so others do not have to step in your stuff in order to find help."

Be very careful of disclosing your intention to conduct a possible intervention at this preliminary stage. Be vague about your concerns. In this brief phone call or personal visit, ask only if they are concerned. You are simply pursuing or evaluating various options at any stage of this dance.

Chapter 3

Family Examples

Let's set up a typical male alcoholic example and the multiplied dances, or negotiations, that happen in his life bringing his concerned others to the point of seeking an interventionist. I will call him Addie and his wife Ann. This family or their acquaintances may think they are dying of the big terminal "U," or terminal uniqueness. This or a similar scenario is going on in one out of every ten families, so it is not unique at all. Some families see the ongoing pattern they are passing on to their children and develop a desire to break this pattern with strong measures such as an intervention.

The story is really affected by Ann's family of origin. Her maternal grandfather died of liver failure. He verbally abused her faithful, submissive grandmother who enlisted her children to protect him from exposure to the church and his community. Ann's mother grew up with the need to clean up, cover up, protect the family, and fix someone with a secret problem. We probably all know someone with this sort of personality. Of course she found such a troubled soul in Ann's father, who also came from a family with addiction issues.

Negotiation dances began many years ago. The family member who was identified with a problem took the position, "I don't need any help. I like the taste of alcohol! My friends and I do this; my father and uncle did not get harassed by their wives for doing just what I do, so leave me alone." The wife and family took the traditional position of "I wish you would cut back. What do I do to drive you to drink so much? You must love alcohol more than me, so I must be driving you to drink, just as you accuse me of doing. Since I am guilty and ashamed of what happens at our home, I must continue to cover this up and try to fix things by myself." His fallback position was, "I'll cut back and only drink at home, just beer or wine. Please don't leave me!" Her fallback position was, "Okay, if you do this I will sleep with you again, will tell the kids to clean up your messes and be quieter, and not to bring friends over to see our troubles. We will be 'just fine, thank you' at church and in public."

So Mom worked with him and then with the kids to cover up and protect him. The kids learned of extra concessions if they went along with the cover-up. They learned to even blackmail parents or other family members to keep the secrets. They negotiated a payoff for acceptance and silence.

The "progressive" (see Progressive illustrations) nature of this problem spirals down (see Spirals section). The disease does not simply "go to hell in a hand basket." The drinking increased until the wife made more threats not carried out; he made more commitments not completed. The kids learned caretaking, rescuing, fixing, covering up, turning the other cheek, going the extra mile, not saying no, and generally using poor boundary skills to survive. This took years of patterned cover-up, negotiation, fallback, compromise, accepting less, and competitive, inadequate, we-are-bad, wrong-answer sort of growth. This describes a family dance, a bad dance, or a process, a bad process.

Is it any wonder that Ann, the daughter from this type of family background, wants to be a nurse or work in some helping field? She may often work in the worst nursing home in town, work holidays, and can't do enough religiously to feel right. She also covers for her children and their peer issues. Does she exhibit poor boundaries and always lose in any dance, process, or negotiation? Isn't she the one always exploited? Doesn't she have a hard time accepting or understanding when others negotiate in a healthy way or even be so bold as to say no to her? Of course she found Addie to clean up after and fix! This was the dance step process, or negotiations, happening in this system generations before someone asked a person like me to try to intervene. In fact, Ann can rarely make the call to initiate the possible intervention. Commonly, a sister-in-law or other detached friend negotiates the beginning of an intervention.

The sister-in-law, or nonenmeshed concerned other, begins a new round of dancing, or negotiations, by stating to Addie's brother that Addie can't drive with their kids again or mess up their family gathering again. He is Addie's brother, had the same family background, and, although not abusing alcohol, wants to stay out of this conflict. He declines to help his wife seek answers for his brother. "Live and let live. We do not need to air our dirty laundry. If you cannot say something nice, do not say anything at all. We do not need to clean someone else's back porch." All these seem like traditional King James Version basic Bible from his family's teachings.

The sister-in-law seeks and finds an interventionist, someone like me. She wants the interventionist to go out and make Addie stop abusing his family and alcohol. This starts another negotiation dance with the interventionist. He cannot and will not attempt to get involved in rescuing Addie alone. Her fallback position is then to "just explain it to me over the phone and I will do this myself." I then try to model healthy boundaries by not doing too much fixing or rescuing over the telephone. Much preparation is needed to be successful.

Some families seek instruction and then decide not to follow up with a formal intervention. I often coach five approaches to consider. (See the Five Options chart.) The major approach is a full-blown maxi-intervention. If we conduct the rehearsed, structured maxi-intervention, nine out of every ten people do accept admission into the suggested level of rehabilitation or therapy.

Over 800 families and concerned groups have trusted me, starting in 1973, to assist them in conducting a caring confrontation for folks, or Addies, with a problem. A trained interventionist can help you enjoy a safe resolution to whatever conflict or behavior problem you are seeing in someone for whom you care.

Actual Interventions

A nationally known treatment center referred a father seeking help for his twenty-nine-year-old daughter for a possible intervention. I'll call her Amy. These facts are accurate, but I disguised her identity. She was a popular cheerleader in college, never married, and fired from a successful job. Her health and appearance had cratered. She'd begun borrowing money from family and friends and had stolen from her maternal grandmother. She'd gone to a concerned other's home to crash for long hours and then disappeared for weeks. She did not carry her driver's license and was paranoid regarding police and getting arrested.

I told the dad to try to gather at least six folks who cared for his daughter. Dad gathered a group of eight, including her ex-fiancée, grandmother, dad's fiancée, two old school friends, a brother, and a sister. We met on two Sunday afternoons to decide if there was a serious problem, how to intervene, and how to get her to meet with the group of concerned others.

I wish I had been the one to come up with a way to get her into a meeting. The way they did this was creative. Dad told her he wanted to have a good time with his daughter and wanted to take her across the state line to a casino to gamble and have fun. He was not lying to her. This was the truth, but he had hopes of getting help. She agreed to go. Because she needed her ID to be able to fly to the treatment center, he told her if she won big bucks, she would need her driver's license for identification, so be sure to bring it. The group and I hid the cars and waited at his home at 3:30 a.m. for their arrival. Dad called at 3:45 to tell us he was coming and was about thirty minutes away.

He had plane tickets for Amy, her ex-boyfriend, and himself, and had prearranged a payment assurance to the treatment center. You can only imagine the shock and anger when she walked into her dad's home to sleep and all these people were there. Her sister had a bag packed in her trunk to carry the other three to D/FW airport. We finished the intervention statements described here with some typical anger and trash talk from Amy. She agreed to go to treatment after some objections, and the four of them went to fly the three away.

She is out of treatment now and attending at least four self-help groups per week. If she is drug free two years later, we will have solid confidence in a clean future.

Her dad reported good compliance with the treatment and follow-up meetings. As a side note, he lost over $900 at the casino to keep Amy there until time to leave to meet us at his home. This family was willing to risk her anger to confront her addiction.

Successful with Three Subjects

I helped a union official carry out three interventions for family members one stormy night. Two siblings and one of their spouses were drugging together. We had prearranged three separate treatment facilities. I do not know of any facility that would allow two family members or close associates to receive treatment at the same time. We gathered a large group of concerned others. We intervened with the single sibling first, and a loved one left with this person to check in at a distant treatment facility. The sibling was next. A grandparent had to gently take a baby out of the arms of this one so others could conduct the intervention. It was beneficial to be able to assure this one that one of their siblings was already on the way to another treatment program. The using spouse was the tough intervention. The group had to use the final stages of consequences, assuring that the other two had already agreed to accept help. The baby had been removed from being around the drugs and would probably need to stay away from this person if not in active recovery. I wish I knew all three were celebrating abstinence and recovery at this writing. The last I heard, the two siblings were in recovery, but the spouse did not stay in the treatment program and remains out of the family and still drugging. Two out of the three are doing well. The large group helping on that stormy night is convinced they had to do what they did and gave appropriate options to all three of the drug users. Of course, we pray the third member is coming to reality and will find help soon.

I helped a family of eight siblings intervene with one cocaine-using sibling that has a master's level professional license. All were afraid to include their older parents, who lived many miles away. The parents were totally unaware that the problems and difficulties their grown child was experiencing were from heavy cocaine use. The other seven siblings feared and grieved telling the parents their most educated child was drugging and that all eight had used together at times. This intervention was successful.

Chapter 4

Serenity Triangle

SERENITY TRIANGLE

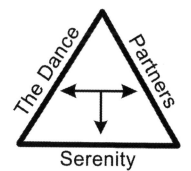

Dance

Partners   **Serenity**

I call the gaining of acceptance of help or treatment by a loved one who refuses help "serenity."

Serenity is not the absence of confrontation. Serenity is dealing with confrontation, using true care and concern with respect and healthy boundaries.

So, I say confrontation is your friend. Resolved conflict is also the friend of your loved ones. How you deal with confrontation can bring family and friends closer than you ever imagined.

I remember this illustration as "DPS." Not the Department of Public Safety, but the *dance*, the *partners*, and *serenity*. This illustration is adapted from a quote from Dr. Randolph Lowery, now president of Lipscomb University, in a lecture on conflict resolution. He called this the "Satisfaction Triangle" using Product, People, and Process as the three legs. The most important leg of the Serenity Triangle is the dance, or process. If we stop the dance, we will never find serenity. Stay in the dance. Do all the steps. Intervention, or any endeavor, is a dance. The purpose of this chapter is to discuss the dance, or process, of getting a loved one to accept direly needed assistance, even if they are reluctant.

Three legs form this triangle.

The Dance or the Process

The Steps of Accomplishing the Goal of Getting Someone You Care for to Accept Viable Available Appropriate Choices.

Five Options

1. You could continue with things just like they have been, with poor boundaries and enabling the behaviors to continue also.

2. All concerned others could simply agree to stop all enabling and victim role-playing. I suggest this pledge: "I'm simply not available to participate in any form of abuse today, and I do not plan to be available tomorrow. No verbal, mental, physical, sexual, substance, family, religious, financial, or self-abuse will happen to me today." A soldier told me to "cut to the chase. Say it all in three words: No diss today!" No disrespect, dishonor, disregard, disown, disgust, discourage, displace, or desertion will occur to me or from me today, and I do not plan to give or take diss tomorrow.

3. A third approach is to have one special person conduct a mini-intervention described in other pages called "Being Heard by an Unwilling Listener." A mini-intervention is simply a setup for a potential maxi-intervention at a later time.

4. A forth option is to conduct a maxi-intervention, which is used after the mini-intervention. I will cover this approach first. I think the mini-intervention will be more powerful and focused if the one attempting it has already studied a possible maxi-intervention that is in reserve if needed.

5. A fifth choice is for concerned others to pledge and carry out continuing consequences if the person they care for refuses assistance. Each participant holds the others accountable for pledges of change. This is similar to "no diss" but with added consequences. If you always do what you've always done, you always get what you always got.

I believe interventions are biblical, decent, moral approaches to communicate with an unwilling listener. Some families seek instruction and then decide not to follow up with a formal intervention.

Other interventionists conduct what some call an "integrated intervention" with the intervenee, totally participating in the preparation and sessions. This works for many, but it is not my background and experience of success.

In this case, our product, or goal, is serenity, when a loved one accepts help. This is a good illustration for approaching any situation or opportunity. If we focus only on the finished outcome, we will not likely find serenity, or peace of heart and mind. If the other two legs of the triangle are the focus, we are much more likely to find serenity with the finished product. You and your loved ones can celebrate serenity as you are assured you have absolutely done all you can at any point of the dance. A successful process or dance does not stop when someone sets a boundary by walking away or taking a break for a while. This is merely a part of the dance or process as we set healthy boundaries in the loved one's best interest. In a conflict, we are still dancing when we declare "I am simply not available to participate in any form of abuse today and actually do not plan to be available tomorrow. Perhaps we can discuss this at great length later." Or to say, "Get back to me later if you want to talk; or if I think of a different idea, I will try to get back to you." Saying, "You could be right" as you look away or walk away from a confrontation, not arguing about a point is to remain in the dance. These can be safe detachments or boundaries to avoid engaging in further abuse. Setting healthy boundaries helps us avoid compassion fatigue.

Partners

Focusing on respect for all the people involved, or the *partners*, is important. Many years ago I asked an elderly Jewish man in South Texas what he attributed his business success to. He said, "Everyone wants to be wanted." His family, customers, staff, vendors, and competitors all want to be wanted. He also said, "Everyone wants to belong to someone and everyone wants someone to belong to them." So one of the three legs of the Serenity Triangle is "P" for partners; we focus on the respect for all the partners involved.

Serenity

I love this Serenity Triangle and will use it as an outline. The Bible speaks of "peace of heart and mind beyond understanding." Even a psychiatrist examining you cannot understand your level of serenity.

Chapter 5

Healthy Boundaries

- **Positive**
- **Negative**
- **Stop Enabling with Healthy Boundaries Reducing Compassion Fatigue**

Do not skip the following discussions of Origins of Boundaries, Balancing Our Boundaries, and the vicious cycle or "TRAPezoid," in which loved ones become entangled. This shape is called a *trapezoid*, or "trap zone" for a group of caregivers. When I try to leave this part off, I always come to regret it and need to go back over this section again. When you try to help anyone with any problem, you cannot help him or her without using healthy boundaries. Like balancing your checkbook or books, you can have positives and negatives, credits and debits. This will help you avoid compassion fatigue or emotional burnout.

I remember this as CCCC's or the eight C's. I do not claim to have this internalized yet. It helps me to go over this illustration two or three evenings per week to relax and to go on with a more balanced life.

Intervention
Reducing Compassion Fatigue

Positive:
- You do Care
- They have Choices
- Consequences
- And Complete
    Responsibility

Negative:
You can't:
- Cure
- Control
- Change
- or Cause the
    problem

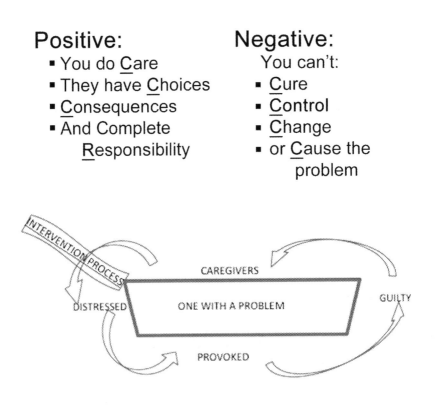

Trapezoid Shape is a team splitting
vicious cycle of Enabling.

Positive C's

The left column is the positive or credit side. For this first C, we do *care* or bring ourselves to have unconditional compassion. Some folks that we try to help with a problem are impossible, or at least hard, to like, let alone love. They may have hurt you or done mean things. He may actually be your enemy. But I believe we must love our enemies. So here is the best I can do, so far, in my efforts with some hard-to-love people: I can come to have unconditional positive regard for their best interest long term.

Counselors notify a client on the first visit of confidentiality issues. Everyone in Texas is required to report any mention of child abuse. When a client came in asking for help to stop molesting a minor, I needed to go over in my mind that I can come to have unconditional positive regard for his best interest long term. I helped him with his request and believe it really is in his best interest long term to stay in prison while the minor grows up. Do I *care* about him unconditionally? Yes.

The second positive C is this: He does have *choices*. He has viable, available, appropriate choices. If he makes responsible choices, better things will begin in every realm of his life. If he makes irresponsible choices, worse things will continue in every realm of his life. Help is possible and available. As caregivers, we try to offer choices in a receivable way.

Thus, he has consequences, the third C. He can make smart choices and gain great consequences. He can make inappropriate choices and will receive painful consequences. The big boys tell me, "Don't do the crime if you can't do the time." This is where many concerned others relapse back into codependency and compassion fatigue. They might use scripts or self-talk such as, "If we had not..., If we had only... If she should have..., We must have..., We could have controlled..." and before long, the concerned other is assuming responsibility for the other person's compulsive behavior. Go over to the last negative C: "I did not *cause* his problem," balancing it with the fourth C: "He is *completely* responsible for his choices. In his best interest long term, leave him completely responsible for his choices.

Negative C's

The first negative C hits me deeply. You or I cannot *cure* him or his problem. A poster we see in support group meetings reads, "There is a Higher Power and YOU ain't Him." There is a God and I am not Him. The reason this hits me, and I need hitting, is, as a counselor, I could get the feeling I am healing some poor soul. This is so untrue. I cannot heal anyone.

The second negative C is just as true. You or I cannot *control* him or his behavior. Even if this is your teenager, you actually cannot control him. This is negative, isn't it?

The third negative C may be hard to accept at first. We cannot *change* him or his problem. Really, can we change someone else?

Well, this is the negative side. If I stop now, it seems like giving up, or a hopeless situation. Addie may try to put this guilt trip upon you, saying "You should...you must...you gotta...you have to..." This simply cannot be true. The last C is the most important principle to reduce compassion fatigue, to stop enabling, to set healthier boundaries: You did not *cause* his problem.

The one we are trying to bring to accept help is in the center of the trapezoid, or trap zone. Typically someone outside the box in the caregiver position helped, rescued, took care of him, fixed him, and served him as a good Christian in the early times of his problems. Helpers and caregivers become susceptible to compassion fatigue or burnout. They may become people pleasers, solving all the problems. For instance, caregiver #1, perhaps his mother, may have covered up some incident to avoid trouble with a sibling or other family member. He promised never to do such again if she would just not get him in trouble for this offense. He let her down and she moved around the upper left corner from caretaker to being the distressed walked-on victim. This is a sharp-pointed corner the first time this happens. It's a jab in the side to feel used, stepped on, door matted, and made his victim.

Next, helper #2, someone else, a sister, dad, or girlfriend offers to rescue him. This second partner simply comes to aid or rescue. Well, I have little doubt this second helper comes to feel used and distressed also.

Mom, or the first helper, sees what is happening and becomes provoked. She moves around the lower left corner. The jab of pain is not as sharp this time. She becomes angry. She says some harsh, disapproving words to the loved ones. Now he becomes angry. Now helper #1, Mom, becomes the perpetrator. She begins as the protector, and becomes the one who hurts his feelings. She moves around the lower right corner and now feels guilty for causing his anger.

The third player, or partner, gets involved in this vicious cycle. He offers a place to stay, pays off tickets or legal issues, and defends the loved one in the middle of all this. Obviously, the one feeling so guilty feels compelled to fix everything with one more attempt, thus crossing around the upper right corner from guilt trip to rescuer again.

You get the picture, I hope. If a problem continues for some time, I know we can find sixty-four helpers, fixers, rescuers, caregivers circling the one with the out-of-control problem. Loved ones are divided. One wants to rescue and cover the issue; their spouse may be at that very moment in a rage of anger. They are split. One sibling may be that day's distressed victim or the one walked on, while another one feels guilty. I see parents of chemical abusers going for divorces over a child who split the family. The problem is manipulative, cunning, and baffling. It divides and splits families and acquaintances in this vicious circle. The problem needs several victims to continue the disease. We put things together, tighten them up by rotating them clockwise, righty-tighty. We take things apart, unscrew them by twisting them off with lefty-loosey. This pattern will tear a family apart, pitting one against the other.

Let me tie this all up. You did not cause his problem. But if you are participating in this pattern of team splitting, you are enabling the problem to continue. You are in the trap zone! How do you get out of this trapezoid pattern? I will cover how to celebrate your recovery later. For now, drawing a line between helping, rescuing, fixing, caregiving, and being walked on, stepped on, used, distressed and playing the victim in any form is in his best interest long term. Memorize this: "I am simply not available to participate in any form of abuse today, and I do not plan to be available tomorrow." No diss today! This includes giving or taking verbal, physical, mental, emotional, spiritual, financial, sexual, chemical, and especially self- abuse. Try to avoid using any form of these four words: should, must, have to, or as we say in Texas, gotta. These can be and most often are used irrationally and for self-abuse.

The one with a problem has a mission to push this line further around the corner, counterclockwise. Your role is to hold the line and define the difference between yes and no. Above the line is Yes, or okay. Below the line is, No, I am not a victim today.

Stop Enabling with Healthy Boundaries

If the sixty-four concerned others cooperate to maintain this line, his chances of recovery are greatly enhanced. Stop all enabling! This is effective. This is the act of loving or caring for them enough to become tough. If only six concerned others stick with this commitment, he stands a good chance of coming to reality. No giving or taking distressing, dishonoring, disrespecting, disowning, or disrupting. In other words, No diss today!

Feeling guilty or shame based does not help you to say no. Feeling clear, clean, and forgiven will help you say no. "The grace of God" teaches us to say no (see Titus 2:11-12, New International Version) This is resisting bad stuff for yourself but can also be "no!" to bad stuff from others.

Recovery Based on Three Truths

For you to encourage the one with the problem to begin healthy boundaries, you yourself must demonstrate or mentor good boundaries. So our recovery is based on these three truths:

1. I am actually a good and lovable person.

2. I have the freedom and responsibility to choose to do something smart today, and I plan to tomorrow.

3. I am simply not available to participate in any form of abuse today and do not plan to be available tomorrow. No diss today!

Helping someone toward recovery from a compulsive behavior is hard, emotionally draining work. As I said earlier, helpers and caretakers become susceptible to compassion fatigue or emotional burnout and feel, why bother? But out-of-control behavior is unlikely to cure itself! The opposite of serenity is compulsivity. Particularly with chemical addiction, the problem is progressive. Let us look at the compulsive behavior from a disease perspective.

Chapter 6

Define the Problem

Some define an issue as a *disease* if it meets the four criteria below:

Four Qualities Define a Problem

1. **Progressive**
2. **Primary**
3. **Incurable**
4. **Fatal**

Think of the person you are considering helping to see if they have a disease, meeting the four criteria. There is debate regarding calling an addiction a disease. Some say we are giving the person an excuse or an out. Is Addie just predisposed to do their addictive behavior and not responsible for his choices? I say no way! Diabetics may be genetically predisposed to their health problem. But when a diabetic is aware of his problem, he is still responsible for eating, exercising, and weight choices. I will illustrate these four characteristics of a problem at some length, especially the first one.

Progressive Problem

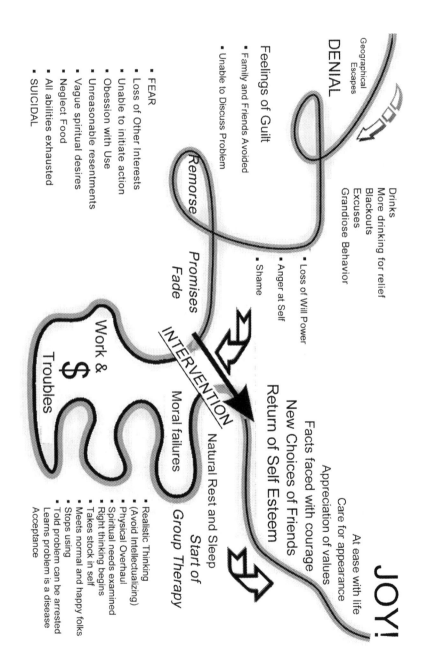

Many years ago E. M. Jelinek studied alcoholism and addictive behaviors. He is said to have given us his valley chart, although he later separated himself from this chart. Among other understandings, he offered the stages of an addiction as going downhill to bottom-out, and then recovery going up and to the right. He helped us realize addiction develops in a predictable path. The apostle Paul described a similar state of affairs when he wrote, "What I want to do I do not do, but what I hate I do" (Romans 7:15, NIV).

I've drawn a more complicated valley chart above showing addiction as not simply developing and progressing in a straight line toward the bottom. Addictive behavior usually begins in a small way, deteriorates, has some consequences, backs off or improves, and levels off at a new acceptable plateau of use. Progress is two steps down and then one step up. It then increases, struggles to back off again to a new lower plateau (not as far up as before), levels off at this new low, then cycles down. The person struggling with a compulsive behavior sometimes works hard to make improvements. He can even abstain for a time. The damaging behavior or addictive problem will get worse if left untreated. Typically folks try a "geo-cure" or geographical escape early in the problem. "Let us just move to California to get away from these problems." When this fails and they move back home, perhaps with some financial assistance, we hear, "We want to get away from this rat race, we could move to Arkansas, raise a few pigs, live the simple, clean life there." Family and friends say, "If he only got away from those bad friends, get new playmates, and new playpens, then things would be better."

Occasional use increases, tolerance increases, and self-esteem decreases. I do not share the old belief that someone must continue down until he hits bottom, because then and only then can we expect him to get help. I believe you can help him see that *now* is the bottom. You can effectively raise the bottom to right now, this day and time. He can get it. This is as far down as you intend to participate in the progress of this illness. Waiting for him to hit bottom may be too late. Some are low-bottom before they accept help. Some folks celebrating recovery were high-bottom, meaning they realized at an early stage of their illness where this could go and sought change.

I do not remember anyone seeking recovery from a serious compulsive behavior without being coerced by an outside influence. Probation may be about to be revoked, or the loss or potential loss of job, family, health, or other impending consequences can help them to see reality. Intervention helps us cut across the valley before he goes down to the pits. See the word *intervention* on the chart above. Also, notice *recovery*, on the right side of the drawing, is not simply a straight vertical line, up, up, and away. Recovery is more than just a Serenity Prayer away. Recovery is fraught with rough times. I cannot find anyone in solid recovery two years after treatment who did not struggle with the steps, the dance, or the process of recovery, attend intensive support groups, acquire a mentor or sponsor, and accept accountability to another human being. Ninety days of abstinence is a huge hurdle. Some professionals see the toxic level drop way down at around ninety days of abstinence. The subconscious brain seems to demand a new supply or set up scenarios of craving incidents around ninety days into recovery. This is similar to a marathon runner's "wall" at about twenty miles, where the body just cannot go on any farther. Practiced, trained runners understand this dynamic and break through this wall to the finish line. With a high level of understanding, support, and encouragement, recovery continues through this ninety-day wall. The greatest milestone of recovery occurs after the joy of completing two years of consistent abstinence. Many slip at anniversaries of ninety days and at two years. Maintaining recovery is much more natural after two years in the recovery process or dance. See illustration of "2750 Cravings"

View of the Progression and Recovery of a Problem

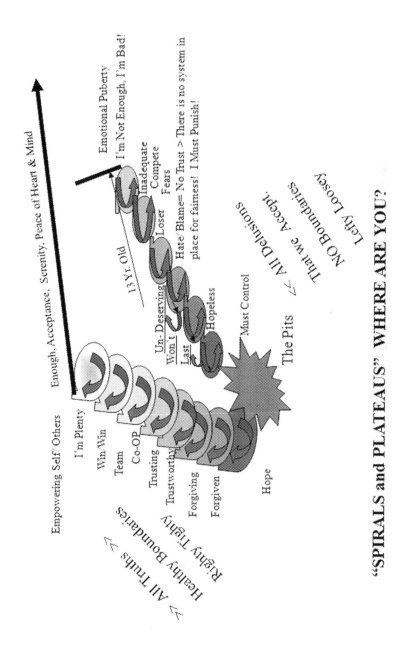

These spirals come from several theories, suggestions, or approaches, all rolled into this sheet. On this illustration look at the thirteen-year-old moving along in life upward and to the right. He is making normal progress. We hope he is maturing socially, mentally, physically, and spiritually. At about thirteen years old, most kids hit a wall or a limit. This is a message that "I am not enough; I'm inadequate; I can't fit in; I'm ill at ease; I'm bad," sort of an overwhelming feeling.

"Teachers don't like me, I can't keep up with the big shots; my clothes are not normal; I'll never fit in with the crowd." He hits this wall and starts to move in a negative direction, down and to the left, the opposite of progress. He moves counterclockwise. He knows he's falling and works hard to reverse his direction and recover. He hits a level of acceptance, abstinence, or recovery, and he learns to live with it. He levels off at this plateau for a while. As he gets older he realizes others are doing better. They seem popular, adjusted, developed—winners. So that means he must be a loser. To him the world appears as a win/lose environment. "There are top dogs and underdogs. This is a dog-eat-dog world. It's every man for himself. The guy who ends up with the most toys wins." He must learn the competitive nature of life. He is not winning. He comes to distrust the winners—authority figures, church, faith, his family—and to fear the system. Paranoia is common through this stage. He blames others for his inability to adjust.

A Marine friend told me, "A thief thinks everyone else is a thief." An untrustworthy person does not trust others. So, does it follow that honest folks are gullible and/or have poor boundaries? He begins to hate the top dogs that get all the goodies while he gets disrespected, discouraged, disapproved, disregarded. Street language covers this. Teens say, "Do not diss me, man!" *They* are the bad guys. He really needs to give *them* "a dose of *their* own medicine. Teach *them* a lesson. Bullies and road hogs need to be pushed back." He becomes the justice system.

Through my teen years I had a huge problem with thinking I must fix the bad guys. I do not like bumper stickers, but I saw a bumper sticker in Saginaw, Texas, that I thought I must have. It would be right in the face of the ugly bumper stickers like "Honk if you love Jesus." What good would it do if a lot of us blared our horns? The sticker that appealed to me for a few minutes said, "If you love Jesus, seek justice; any fool can honk!" There, that is what I needed to tell them! Then I realized, this is one of my old problems. I thought again of getting even, with me being the justice system, punishing the wrongdoers. I am not the Old West posse that must saddle up and ride after the outlaws.

See the illustration of yet another spiral downward and leveling off, and plateauing with a new comfort zone. Addie feels guilty, full of shame, disappointed in his lack of positive progress. He again believes he should be punished, and get what is coming to him. He must not enjoy the good life since he is actually a lowlife.

He works to reverse this cycle and recovers to a point and levels off at this plateau. He says, "This may be as good as it gets." He fights his spiraling fall, turns it upward and to the right, in a clockwise direction. He did not realize there is a nonglare glass ceiling just above his head. He bonks into it and turns back down. This ceiling is the old message, "Even if you get things going better, the good times will not last. You will fail again and really get hurt this time." He tries so hard again and hits the second invisible ceiling: "You are bad; you do not deserve to have the good life. You will soon get what's coming to you. Give up!" These two ceilings are deep-seated paradigms by now. They quickly become self-fulfilling prophecies and turn out to be his perception and then become his reality.

As life goes on, he feels such a loss of control. He can't gain control of any realm of his life. This leads to someone who acts very controlling. When we see some people with a compulsive need to straighten everyone else out, get the rest of us to behave to their high standards, even to controlling the order of cans and stuff on a shelf, we might come to believe this person is dealing from a base of inadequacy or "not enoughness." As you come across someone in a neighborhood, an office, a family, or group who seems bossy and controlling beyond their station or responsibility, then you are probably looking at someone with low self-esteem, with a core paradigm of "I'm not enough!" Thus, through abuse, rage, bullying, and walking over others' rights, he will try to gain control of at least this part of his life. But it is really the loss of control.

Below this plateau is another level of despair. This is the loss of hope. Deep depression, zero joy, suicidal thoughts and actions may follow. He has bottomed out. This counterclockwise spiraling downward and to the left all begin with a lie. He bought the lie of "I'm bad or not enough!"

This is the basic lie of all declines and results in very poor boundaries. He no longer can say no in any situation. The more he gets walked on, the more he attracts abusers. He is both controlling and victimizing others while at the same time being dominated by others. Showing poor boundary skills, he is known as a good old boy who will give the shirt off his back. He'll give up time for himself and time with his family and his self-care.

Former First Lady Nancy Reagan led a campaign to "Just say no" to drugs. This was a nice slogan and brought awareness of abuse, but I never saw anyone involved in drugs be able to hear this slogan and "just say no." Maybe it was a campaign for the kids to say no and just not begin. When you are a bad boy and getting a dose of guilt and shame, this does not help. Every one of us probably deserves to be tied up to a pole in front of a large auditorium and punished for some past behaviors. Everyone coming out the door could beat us with a stick. Would this help our self-control?

Is this not the same big lie given to Adam, King David, Jesus in the wilderness, our teenagers, and to every one of us from the evil one? A person addicted to pornography or other compulsive behaviors is probably feeling a lack of enoughness in their life. The Bible teaches us the exact opposite in verses like "I am convinced you are full of goodness, complete in knowledge, and competent to counsel others"

There is a great biblical instruction on how to say no! Let me quote "It teaches us to say no to godless ways and sinful longings. We must control ourselves. We must do what is right. We must lead godly lives in today's world. That's how we should live as we wait for the blessed hope God has given us." (Titus 2:11-13, NIRV).

What is the "it" that teaches us to say no to? It is not shame and guilt. Here is more of the quote:

"We are waiting for Jesus Christ to appear in all his glory. He is our great God and Savior.... He wanted to make us pure. He wanted us to be his very own people. He wanted us to long to do what is good." (Titus 2:11-14, NIRV).

Look at a clean white page from down in the stack of printer paper, untouched by human hands, a pure pristine, virgin, unmarked innocent page. Can we have a record this unblemished? No ink beside our name? Is it humanly possible for any of us to get this clean? No way. This process is not for sale. We cannot earn it. We do not draw names to exchange gifts for this one. Realizing this purity somehow teaches us to say no! Read the rest of the rest of the story: "Those are the things you should teach. Cheer people up and give them hope. Correct them with full authority. Don't let anyone look down on you" (Titus 2: 15, NIRV).

This is the bottoming out that may lead to turning a life around into recovery.

Now Start to Celebrate Recovery

Now we are on the left side of the Spiral Chart, moving upward, to the right, spiraling clockwise. This will lead to healthy boundaries. This is the balance of boundaries to say yes at the appropriate time and no when that is in the best interest.

This is the start of hope vs. hopelessness on the downward spiral. This is putting it back together. Typically, when I meet with concerned others regarding change, confrontation, setting new boundaries and consequences, and avoiding compassion fatigue, the question of suicide comes up. Is suicide the total lack of hope?

Where do we get hope? Not from counselors or others, really. Here is the actual source of hope: "May the God of hope fill you with all joy and peace as you trust in him, so that you may overflow with hope by the power of the Holy Spirit. I myself am convinced, my brothers and sisters, that you yourselves are full of goodness, filled with knowledge and competent to instruct one another" (Romans 15:13-14, NIV).

We remember which way to tighten or loosen bolts and nuts by the saying "lefty-loosey" and "righty-tighty." The downward spiral is counterclockwise, or lefty-loosey. Things are progressively coming undone, falling apart. This compares to the upward spiral, clockwise or righty-tighty, progressively coming together, caring and sharing, celebrating recovery.

Compare the downward counterclockwise spiral to the upward, clockwise spiral of recovery.

Forgiven vs. Guilt and Shame
Forgiving vs. Hate and Blame
Trustworthy vs. Untrustworthy
Trusting vs. Distrust and Fear

I will teach you how to cut across this spiraling valley with an intervention.

Another View of a Progressive Problem
Seeking Normal Feelings

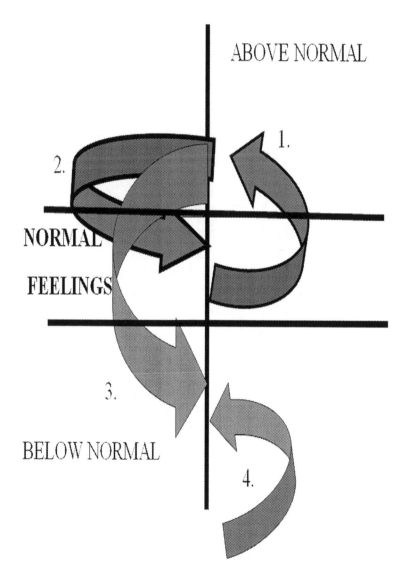

A person heading toward a problem is simply going through normal feelings. He may become ill at ease, uncomfortable, agitated, out of sorts; get the heebie-jeebies, angry, sad, down in the dumps, or whatever. He does not like the way he feels.

First, #1 on the drawing above, a drink, a drug, a gamble, sex, stopping medication, increasing medication, pigging out on food, buying something, trying retail therapy, or doing something out of the norm will at least change the way he feels for a little while.

In an hour or so, he returns to feelings in the mid or normal range. This is #2 on the drawing. No big harm done. This relief will work at times or for a while. We all seek some escapism occasionally, sometimes appropriate, recreational escapes; sometimes inappropriate, harmful activities. As this did work to give at least a change in unpleasant feelings, doing more might work better. If one drink helped a little, two drinks will change the feeling even more. Thus comes the increase of treating self to some changed feelings, whether this is a change to pleasant feelings or to unpleasant feelings.

The activity continues until he ends up feeling below normal at #3 below. Perhaps he can use his escape enough to just get back to feeling normal again, no longer getting any euphoria or good vibes from use.

He will come to the point where he cannot use enough to even feel normal. This is the miserable state of #4 on the chart. Look at the progressive pattern of a compulsive behavior. It started off working for a while; then he needed more to help, failed, and finally, no matter how much he used, it no longer worked for him.

I ask groups in treatment to tell me when they first took any mind-altering chemical, alcohol, marijuana, pills, or other drugs. In every group of ten or more, the average age of first usage is now twelve, moving down from thirteen years old a few years ago. The common entry to all addictions is nicotine, alcohol, and marijuana. I've never met someone wanting to become an addict. No one aspires to someday fail to find a place to get a needle in and finally resort to injections in their groin or foot. Compulsive behavior is progressive and the opposite of serenity if left unaddressed. Compulsive behavior is *so* treatable, if treated.

If alcohol was just discovered this year, and we knew where it leads, it would be outlawed and feared more than cocaine or heroin. The physical, mental, relational, and financial harm to all of us is greater by far from alcohol than from all the other mind-altering chemicals combined. When a mind-altering chemical processes through the blood, brain, liver, and elimination system, the addictive nature cannot distinguish which chemical gave the turn-on. To the dependent's brain, a drug is a drug. Alcohol is a mind-altering drug. A drug is a drug. All addicts have a drug of choice, but all drugs, including alcohol, turn on or turn back on, the physical and/or mental need for using again. Alcohol was not discovered just this year. People have abused and become dependent on alcohol for thousands of years. Society, religious use, lobbyists, politicians, and even most of our leaders all encourage use of alcohol.

A young person typically gets an overwhelming feeling of inadequacy or of not being acceptable. His performance is lacking, underdeveloped, not enough. He is trapped, uncomfortable, agitated, cross, sick, ill at ease, not normal, or dis-eased. A peer suggests this feeling will be different if he tries a little toke of marijuana or a drink. Sure enough, the first time to use does spark a better feeling, or at least a different feeling. This works. If one drink helps, next time two drinks might feel even better or stronger. He feels better than normal, inhibitions are lowered, and shyness goes away. He learns that in about an hour he may return to feeling normal with few or little consequences. Thus, increased usage progresses. As time goes on, he feels worse than normal after using. He uses more to get back to feeling normal. Later, he cannot even use enough to get back to feeling normal again. He may not be chasing the euphoric feeling of early partaking; he may be simply frustrated in trying to use enough to feel like a normal human being. He is hooked. This describes the progressive nature of this illness.

Primary Problem

The primary problem is the second of the four qualities defining a problem:

1. It is a progressive problem.
2. It is the primary problem.
3. It is an incurable problem, but treatable.
4. It is a fatal problem, if left untreated.

When a person is struggling with a compulsive behavior, someone will say, "If only his wife would quit nagging or—; if she could just be a little more—; if the economy had only—; if his job didn't—; if the authorities had not—; if that tragedy had happened to anyone else—; if his ex had never spent—; if his mom would've just—; then he certainly might have chosen to—." A cruel bad joke about blame says, "If it's not one thing it's your mother".

In truth, addiction is the primary problem. Financial problems, issues, sexual concerns, family conflicts, lack of trust, spiritual worries, physical illnesses, emotional distress, legal and authority stresses, or rage and anger disorders will not improve until this primary problem is resolved and recovery is well along.

That is why I like to work with chemical dependency issues. The very day someone stops using, becomes abstinent, gets into recovery, every aspect of his life improves. If he continues to use, every aspect of his life continues to crater.

Whatever the problem, *it* becomes the primary problem, the main thing.

Here are two accurate clichés:

1. The main thing is to keep
the main thing
the main thing.

2. The main thing is not
a thing!

Buying something, spending money, owning a better house, car, or pool, will not fix this issue.

A wise elder said, "If it can be fixed with money, then it is not that bad of a problem. Some problems cannot be fixed with money, and these are serious." Addiction cannot be fixed with money.

Safe Trees To Tag Up

One or more out of every ten are chosen genetically to play the Game of Life tagged as "it."

Do you remember as a kid playing chase, tag, or It, in the yard? You can be tagged if you are caught off base. Kids argue, "You didn't tag me; I'm not "it"; I was on a base." Nine of every ten are not chosen to play in this game of chase or playing It.

"It" is the pull, the urge, thought, craving, Jonesing, (street talk for craving) desire, to do his compulsive inappropriate behavior. If he plays It on the treeless Wal-Mart parking lot, he will soon get tagged. He has no safe tree to tag up to. If he plays It down in the woods at the golf course, he will have many safe trees to tag up and can jump from safe tree to safe tree and avoid being touched by the "it" for the whole game. Most folks with a compulsive behavior cannot list more than two places or situations where they feel safe from relapse. Only if he establishes safe bases or harbors does he stand any chance of avoiding relapse. It will be with him for life but will become a smaller "it" as he plays the game of life sanely, safely, and in abstinence.

Sand traps will be in the game at best. These include "old playmates and old playpens." After a couple of years in the game, his recovery will take root. Another will look to him to mentor or sponsor them in the game as their safe tree to tag. He will know he is in recovery after two years as he is passing it on to someone else. You cannot keep it if you do not give it away. It is the primary problem.

PROGRESSIVE, PRIMARY, AND NOW
INCURABLE ISSUE

INCURABLE NATURE
OF THE PROBLEM

1/10   9/10

PROBLEM   NO PROBLEM

At least one out of every ten folks in any group has a problem with compulsive behavior, alcohol, or drugs, etc. So nine out of every ten do not have such a problem. Think of a list of 100 doctors, plumbers, nurses, painters, ministers, airline employees, or teachers. Ten or more of this group typically have a progressive compulsive behavior problem, unless they are celebrating their recovery on a daily basis. If these ten with a problem could only join the other ninety without a problem, then they would experience a cure. The research and pharmaceutical industry could get wealthy if they developed something to help an alcoholic to drink a little bit and stop just as ninety of a hundred folks possibly can. This would be such a breakthrough. So we can rightly say, this is an incurable problem. Treatment, remission, and recovery are available. but as with diabetics, those with the problem are not cured, but they can participate in their own best quality of life with a conscientiously applied program of recovery.

Starvation is not curable. Each is responsible to apply a regular regimen of treatment to the deadly condition of starvation. Hundreds of thousands, some of them my dearest friends, are in successful recovery today.

One of the major providers of healthcare benefits surveyed thousands of clients they had spent money on for treatment They did not find any success stories of clients who did not follow up with support group involvement.

Progressive, Primary, Incurable, and Fatal Issue

Left untreated, this illness will kill. Physical, family, spiritual, moral, financial, sexual, esteem, self-worth, ambition, separation, and mental deterioration issues follow addiction.

Years ago, someone urged me to go to a big church tent meeting to hear the elderly black preacher, R. N. Hogan, from California speak. I can recall his booming, shaky voice saying, "This stuff will take you *further* than you want to go, keep you *longer* than you want to stay, and cost you *more* than you want to pay!"

I've read insurance company statements showing addiction taking an average of ten to seventeen years from life expectancy. Someone addicted to alcohol or other drugs, to gambling, pornography, raging, as well as those refusing appropriate level of care, assisted living, medication compliance, and necessary help to survive could fit into all these patterns.

Chapter 7

The Pain of Change

Pain Scale

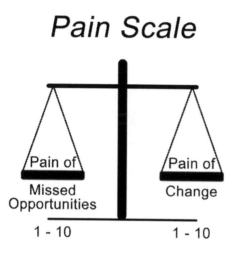

When the pain of Missed
Opportunities is greater the
the Pain of *Change*, then,
and only then are you ready
for *Change!*

Comes with a Measure of Pain

We remember the symbol *pi* from math. This Greek letter is used in math dealing with formulas with circles. Another Greek letter, *delta*, is used to signify difference or change. Delta Airlines used this symbol. Here we are discussing delta to mean difference or change.

Symbol △

DELTA SYMBOLIZES CHANGE

The group of concerned others wants things to change. They want behaviors, actions, thoughts, and events to change or to delta.

Like the old adage says:

> If you always do what you always did,
>
> You always get what you always got.
>
> For changing thoughts and thus behaviors,
>
> You may not be what you think you are,
>
> But what you think,
>
> You are.

A decal on windows of some support group meeting places is a triangle in a circle. Sometime the three sides have the letters H, O, W around them. These are the tenants of recovery: Honesty, Openness, and Willingness. This symbol is also on the book covers and literature of some support groups. I see this triangle as the symbol for change. Some steering wheels have spokes touching the outer rim at three points, making a triangle or delta. I see a steering wheel with a triangle inside as a symbol of the change in direction. You can kick the tires, twist all the other parts of the vehicle, talk to the vehicle until you turn blue in the face, but it will not change direction until you deal with the steering wheel, the symbol and instrument of change in direction.

Remaining at the height or depth (whichever) of despair, insanity, or irrationality is keeping on doing the same things and expecting different results.

We must seek a delta, or change. Do you know someone addicted to alcohol or other drugs, gambling, pornography, or raging, or a person refusing an appropriate level of care, needing assisted living or to comply with medication or necessary help to survive?

Do you feel guilty for letting this go any further? Has anyone suggested you are an inappropriate caretaker, rescuer, and enabler?

His Feeling of Coersion is Good

Intervention will, and should, feel to him like the group ganged up on him and coerced him into treatment against his will. The therapist or treatment facility will have a chance to tell him how much the group cared for him as the days of recovery progress. Almost everyone I've seen enter a program that offers recovery was angry at the intervening group for at least three or four days. It would not be effective to have a proposed future therapist be part of the initial intervention because of this anger issue. I worked in an in-patient treatment facility for almost ten years. After about a week of therapeutic groups it is typical for a patient to say to the group, "Wow! I thought I didn't need to be here with you guys. I think I may have a similar problem as some of you. I can't believe how much my friends and family must love me to lay it on the line and bring me here for help. I'm even more fortunate than some of you who have already lost your families."

Chapter 8

Taking a Roller Coaster Ride

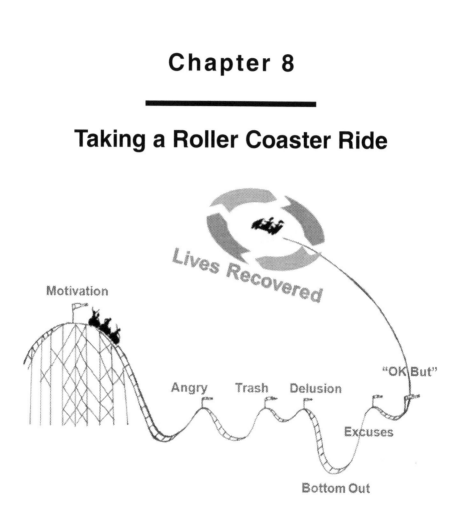

Six Hurdles to Get Past

Trying to help someone who refuses help causes a roller coaster of emotions, with six flags, hurdles, or hills to get over.

1. **Motivation.** First, you have to be motivated to help. That first long hill on a roller coaster is the most fearsome. Don't think, "Why am I doing this? Maybe this is a mistake to

take this ride." The most difficult challenge is the first: to get a group of people on board. If six or more people gather with real firsthand observations of troubling behavior, the remainder of the ride is all downhill; it gets easier.

2. **Anger**. He will be feared by you and probably angry.

3. **Trash**. He may attack with trash talk and say, "You all think I have a problem? What about her there? She does a lot worse than I do. Get on her case before trying to control me!"

4. **Delusion**. He believes he is behaving okay. The obstacle is his denial, his real perception that there is no big deal.

   He may bottom out and even cry when you break through this delusion. You may think he is ready to join you in a recovery or treatment program.

5. **Excuses**. The group needs to predict or elicit up to five excuses why he will not accept the suggested avenue of help.

6. **Okay but later.** This is the last hill to climb. I am sure he will say, "Okay, I will receive help, but later, after the New Year, or whatever."

The greatest problem is to keep him in the dance, the process, the cycle of support groups, and recovery. Gaining acceptance of treatment is simply the start of his celebration of recovery. This is not finished and does not have an ending or a cure.

Recovered lives is a process and not a finished product.

To arrive at the recovery stage, I will discuss scripts and steps to cover every one of these hills.

Chapter 9

Preparing for a Maxi-intervention

This chapter deals with the real meat of an intervention. I usually decline to assist an intervention with less than six participants having firsthand personal observations of disconcerting behaviors. With less than six the chance of success goes way down. I am sure a brief mini-intervention with only one person will yield better results than with two or three trying to convince a reluctant loved one to accept direly needed help.

The proposed participants that are motivated and invested in the intervention need these sheets at the end of this book:

Intervention Scripts
Script to Predict His Five Excuses
Derail Interruptions
Trust-Building Sign-In Sheet

If we are not sure of an attendee's commitment to do an intervention, giving them these papers may scare them off. Judgment is needed to decide who needs how much information to give in advance of discussing an intervention.

Someone *must* check out available treatment, assessment and admission procedures, insurance, and his company's policies regarding time off for treatment, job security, and transportation.

Rehearsal Meeting

Both the rehearsal and especially the actual intervention need to be held without interruption. I always begin with a prayer, unless there is an indication this is offensive. Before we can help someone else, we need good boundaries. If we are conducting a formal intervention, there may be a family system with boundary issues.

Navigating a time and place to rehearse an intervention without interruption is most important. I began discussing a possible intervention with eleven family members in East Texas.

About thirty minutes into the meeting, Addie's fiancée brought her into the house. He had told her what was going on. We just went ahead with the practicing session. I asked around the room, "Why do you love her or care for her specifically? What have you seen or heard, time and place specific, that concerns you? How did you feel, in one word, when you saw or heard her?" This rough intervention actually worked out for the best interest of Addie. (Some interventionists practice doing interventions with the proposed client in the meetings from the start. This is just not my experience.) She did go with her brother to enter treatment. This was a dangerous Intervention because of lack of control. Unpredictable statements might be made that bring harm or libelous words to the endeavor.

Gathering six or more willing participants may be difficult at the first meeting. The orientation meeting(s) are just as important as the intervention itself. The interventionist may discuss healthy boundary issues and several choices.

Excuses Hurdle Script

The group will together write five probable reasons for rejecting help, agree on responses, and assign the one to field each objection with an understanding solution to the objection. This sheet is included at end of this book.

Consequences Script

If he still refuses to accept help, the next phase of the dance or process begins. The interventionist uses the word *change* several times in the next few sentences: "Your loved ones met earlier and pledged to one another some major changes. Whether you join them in change or not, they are holding each other accountable to keep these promised changes. I ask each one to tell you of their individual changes now."

Each one refers to their earlier incident and states a new behavior if there is no treatment or change. As an example, a little nine-year-old girl said, "Daddy, I told you I was embarrassed when I brought friends home and you were in your underwear and drinking and pee'd on the couch. I'm just a little girl. All I can do if we do not get help is to never have any friends come to our house again."

All the partners or participants then give their pledge of change: "I will not bail you out; travel with you; continue to live with you; pay your expenses; listen to your sad stories; allow the children to ride with you or be with you," etc.

As soon as the last one finishes (ranked from the least emotional first to the most emotional statement last), the facilitator or interventionist says, "Since these loved ones are pledging these changes, they simply want you to join them in change by going with them to get help. Will you go with them now?" Nine out of ten people above age twenty will go to treatment by this point.

When and if Addie flat refuses to go, either with or without offering excuses, he may be ready to run away. At any point in the maxi-intervention, if he moves to leave, the interventionist will attempt to avoid his exit by saying several more change statements.

"Your loved ones have already made some commitments to change. Several things are changing. We are simply requesting that you join us in change. Before you leave this meeting, we want you to listen a few more moments as we reveal the commitment for change. The interventionist will cue the first speaker as the group follows in the same order as the original statements.

"Because I care for you, be aware I will not continue bailing you out, (paying for your phone, insurance, rent, probation, food, loans, debts, allowing you to live here, keep or drive the kids, use my stuff) because that makes me part of your problem. I have already pledged to all the others here to stop my enabling activity right now. I'm making this change because I care for your best interest long term. We sincerely request you join us in our recovery from our mutual problem.

The interventionist again asks him to go with the escort to continue this healing process. Each participant will follow suit with their consequence or change statement. This will end with the person with the most significant change.

"If you do not join us in seeking help for our pain, that is certainly your right. Because I care for your best interest long term, you are being served a court order and will not be allowed to hurt me or the kids again. I've committed with these other folks to maintain our resolve to not be part of your destructive behavior from this day forward."

Contingency Plan

You will not use a contingency statement in many cases. This is really a last-gasp effort. Do not jump to this option until you are totally resigned that all other offers are finished. If Addie, the intervenee, flat refuses all offers of change or help, but says he will take care of the issue his way, you might consider a contingency plan.

"Great, Addie, we are glad you are taking care of this your way. We understand you are going to go to some AA meetings on your own to stay sober and clean. Your loved ones here are proud you are doing that for yourself. May your sister-in-law just write down what you agreed to do, so we can leave with some conclusion and satisfaction of this time together? Sister, write this down on your pad there:

"On (date), Addie agrees to attend four AA meetings per week—No, no, Addie, one meeting will not assure the group. Please let her write 'four meetings per week.' Continue, sister. On (date), Addie agrees to attend four AA meetings per week for ninety days and remain abstinent. He will obtain a temporary sponsor at the AA meeting within two weeks.

His family and friends commit to support him and not sabotage his plan during this time. "Now, Addie, so we can all pledge support of our plan, let us pass this around and all sign off on your plan."

"Before we pass this around, please write in, "If Addie might fail in his plan to get help his own way, he agrees to follow up with a more intensive treatment, such as the one suggested here today."

Pass this page around for everyone to sign, with Addie being the last to sign. As an interventionist, I try to know when and where the next local recovery group meets, hopefully a noon meeting. The interventionist, or one of the group, can say, "Fine plan. I want to go with you to your first meeting today. The group meets at noon. Let's go." Addie may go but probably will refuse to go today, or you will learn later that he did not keep the signed commitment.

If he refuses to go to his agreed support group today or even later, the interventionist or family member can say, " Well, we might as well cut to the chase or go on to the suggested treatment program today instead of waiting until later. Let us please simply go on there now."

So, we are simply still in the dance or process.

Specific Details

Next, specific details of the intervention should be determined.

The Place

The place to meet is ultraimportant. Ideally, choose a quiet and private place, such as a den or living room of a concerned other. In the past, we agreed to go to the intervenee's home because he could not be urged to meet anywhere else. But he can order some or all of the participants out of his home or office. I was ordered out of a doctor's home with a loaded gun. His minister, two other medical professionals, wife, and children were ordered out with me. On that occasion, his minister sat down and began the rehearsed lines. The drinking doctor started counting, 10-9- 8...and we all ran from his home. Since then, I refuse to try to intervene where there are known guns and threats on site and when we know he is drunk at that hour. He apologized to everyone a week later and is now in successful recovery for his alcoholism.

A spouse or other family member may say, "Please, these are our guests. I've invited them here; please hear us out." Or, "I've invited this counselor here to help me with an issue; please let us listen." A doctor's, lawyer's, or other professional office, or conference room is okay, but not as relaxed as a home setting to negotiate such a family-oriented and life-changing decision. The invitation to come to a meeting must be filled with honesty. It will backfire to invite him to a party or to discuss a business deal, and then when he arrives shout, "Surprise, you are on *Candid Intervention*." We do not have to be all revealing to set this up. The most likely one can invite him to come over, saying, "I need to discuss something very important at 8:30 this morning. Will you come over now?"

The Time

Pick the time Addie is most sober and might be available. If the optimum time before he starts drinking or using his substance of choice is 4 a.m., then the life-and-death importance of this effort requires you to gather for a 4 a.m. maxi-intervention. Air transportation, check-in times, and the best available escort to go with Addie, and participants available all figure into the timing. If the old high school coach or old youth minister can only come on Sunday morning, then arrange for them to help. If a Sunday morning intervention is the best or only possible time, but the arranged program of treatment cannot start or admit until Monday morning, this is a problem. He may agree to go simply to get you to leave him alone. He can renege on his agreement to go to treatment later or the next day. You could get the escort and him on a plane to the city near treatment to spend the night to continue the dance. This will help avoid his backing out. To do the best possible intervention, strategically avoid each and every obstacle possible.

Cars

The cars are hidden so he will come on in and not drive away in anticipation of a confrontation. Have the car to drive him to treatment or the airport ready and close. Do not stop on the way for gasoline or to make phone calls. I watched a man back out of going on to the treatment facility when his escort driver returned to the house to give someone else their keys. If at all possible, prepack him enough clothes and toiletries for a day-or-two stay. Sometimes buying a few articles to have ready works best rather than attempting to gather some of his own stuff. Hide this bag in the escort's car. You can ship him more clothes that evening or the next day.

Seating

Having a special seating arrangement helps the dance go smoothly. If the big room has scattered chairs, move them in closer so you can talk quietly. Rank the statements from least emotional toward the most tearful statements for order of presentation and eye contact arrangement. The order of speaking must not be consecutive around a circle to avoid him predicting who will speak next.

Seating around a table works best, with everyone able to make eye contact. Try not to let Addie sit on a couch with others. Sitting between two loved ones on a couch may give him a bond or confidence that I do not want him to feel. Place a chair for him around the circle toward the door you expect him to enter. A lonely chair facing the solid group will give Addie the lonely sense I want him to feel. He will more likely remain at the intervention if he realizes he can exit and no one is blocking him from running away.

Placing participants between him and the door sets up a "fight or flight" feeling. We are *not* trapping him, restraining him, or requiring him to stay and listen. Two ex-wives sitting on a couch together, his divorced parents together, his wife sitting between his parents or two of his brothers, his children beside a strong uncle, or his mother with his friend and someone he used drugs or alcohol with in the past sends a strong image of solidarity to him.

Order of Reading Statements

The next few pages are the heart of intervention preparation. I want the subject to sense the collaboration, conspiracy, and cohesiveness of the group. Long love letters are inappropriate and will not receive attention. Short bullet-point statements will get attention. Practice the order of reading these statements, beginning with the least emotional and finishing with the most emotional. Entice him to stay and hear all statements read. He feels he can weather the earlier milder words.

Review all the written scripts from the Typical Script section. Some are deeply emotional and may be read with hesitations and tears. Some are statements of facts and observations. The interventionist will help the group to rank-order the emotional depth of each script. If the most emotional statement is read first, he will likely leave, not able to bear the pain. So the reader with the least emotional statement goes first, second, third, etc., until the most emotional statement is read last. He may roll his eyes on the first or second statement, thinking this will be a piece of cake to resist these silly concerns. Each reader will know who they follow and their closing words. Each reader will practically step on the preceding person's sentence. The group will present all these statements as a cohesive package, running them all together.

Try very hard to keep him from interrupting or debating with any reader's statement of facts. He will probably interrupt at least twice, as discussed elsewhere. Overly prepare and practice for likely contingencies of objections from him. He will interrupt these twelve statements from the participants. The interventionist will assign two or more concerned others to handle these expected interruptions.

The more emotional statement readers will sit straight across from him but will read their statements last. The less gut-wrenching statements are read first and move toward the most painful revelations or painful observations. The rationale for this is to get him to stay until the end.

At rehearsal it will be easy to decide which statement is the most emotional. Each one does not need to know the order of speaking but simply who to follow. Very importantly, the group should practice starting their statement quickly as the reader before them finishes. Addie shouldn't see a break that might allow him to start disputing or giving rationale for his quoted behaviors. If the most tearful statements were read first, he would probably bolt and run away, avoiding any further exposure in front of the concerned folks that are confronting him. Often, a daughter or spouse has the last heavy statements to read.

You will have twelve independent incidents of disturbing observed behaviors. I wish we could go around the circle and read them one at a time and then go back around the circle and read our second incident, but that offers too many chances for interruptions. So each reader must give both their statements back to back. For instance, "I care because…; I saw when you…; I felt…; I need help for this feeling. I also care for you because…; I saw…. He may get comfortable with the milder initial statements and not be ready to weather the facts and memories revealed toward the end. The interventionist can sit to the side. The interventionist doesn't need as much eye contact at first.

I coached a large group of siblings and their parents from New England. They came down to help their lawyer-daughter. As we entered the home where she was staying, I was at the back of the line to go in. I could hear a clamor and loud arguing inside. The elderly dad took me too seriously about not letting her sit on the couch between two supportive family members. He was tugging on his daughter to get her to move off her own couch before we could start. She refused and was amazed that her dad came all the way to Fort Worth to tug on her to make her move from her own couch. We allowed her to stay on the couch between her two siblings, and within an hour she self-admitted to a treatment program. This was not a deal breaker to allow her to sit where she wanted. Normally, we are all seated when the person with a problem arrives in the room. We lose much control when it is necessary to do an intervention on Addie's turf or home.

Touching and Hankies

A quick handshake or brief hug is all you need when Addie arrives. A prolonged greeting time allows him to establish his resistance. I do not know of anyone with a serious problem simply choosing to seek help without some coercion or consequence facing them. I am not reluctant to coerce a person with a deadly illness into accepting an appropriate level of care. Everyone hold your own hankie or Kleenex. If he or anyone else is blubbering with emotion, do not offer a Kleenex, a pat, or a hug. If a hug or hankie would fix the problem, you would not need to be doing a maxi-intervention. I would not want one false tear, fake emotion, or exaggerated statement, but he needs to see the real pain caused by his choices and behaviors. When he nods or agrees to go with the escort to a program of treatment, a quick round of hugs, "I'm proud of you" statements, and good-byes are all you want. Do not bake a batch of cookies, allow long preparations, packing, going by to pay off debts on the way, or calls to friends.

Long delays, from hearing the "Yes, I will go with you" to the treatment place you arranged, to the actual admission are avenues for backing out.

Typical Written Statements

Find the intervention script page in the back and give each person a copy. Writing this script out and having it in each one's lap helps tremendously. I decline to assist an intervention with less than six participants having firsthand personal observations of disconcerting behaviors. With less than six, the chance of success goes way down. I am sure a brief mini-intervention with only one person will yield better results. In many cases the initial caller tells me the problem is a closely kept secret and the caller could not possibly find six willing participants. I hear statements such as, "We cannot call his mom, dad, sister, daughter," etc. Often I gather with two or three and go over the plan and need for more helpers. Almost always there are neighbors, ex-wives, and ex-fellow employees, and/or community folks to call to see if they are concerned or know of an incident that could be relevant.

Hearsay statements are not allowed. Judging, assessing the issue, labeling, blaming, and raised voices will not fit into a successful intervention. No one is allowed to say, "You are an alcoholic. You drink too much. You must take your medication. You must go to the rehab center. You make me angry. We are going to make you get treatment or check you into a nursing home."

Notice the sentences prepared to read are all "I" statements. "I care for you; I saw; I felt; I need help for my fears…" They are sing-song type similar sentences. I want Addie to see this as a conspiracy. Everyone is in co-hoots, and he will see the preparedness of these read sentences.

The sentences come in sets of four. Again, these are "I" statements, not "you" statements. Statements include:

I (care) for you because... (short reason)

I saw or heard you say... (a time and/or place fact)

I felt... (hurt, angry, disgusted, disappointed—your feeling)

I want you to join me in finding help for my pain.

If twelve concerned others with firsthand painful observations are ready, each person will only read one incident. If six are ready, each person will read two incidents. In other words, I require twelve firsthand observations of stressful behavior. I will not allow anyone without a script to sit in or observe the process.

A brother once said he would not tell the family what he wanted to say before the intervention. He had some serious gut-wrenching stories to reveal to his addictive brother. But I declined to go with the group if everyone had not already rehearsed the statements to be read. Everyone in the group must know what will be read and not be shocked or disavow the statements. Many times a loved one will need to quote some foul vulgar words the addict has used. This is the time for his dear sweet mom to say what he called her while he was under the influence. This will add to the gravity of the occasion for him to hear his mom repeat his bad language.

You will not be a party to spreading these stories to a person who hasn't suffered along with the group or is unwilling to take a role. Each one furnishes a forum for the others to read their statements. Each one must hear and agree to the statements. No one will be a part of some libelous or damaging words to be held against them later. If one strays from the script and makes a damaging remark, all are guilty of being part of this forum. Each has a different story to reveal, and at the end, the stories are all on the table so the group can share and see the mutual pain. I discuss elsewhere the legal risk of being part of a forum with inappropriate statements being read or blurted out. The "More is less, and less is more" rule fits here. Some interventionists want a longer letter written out, read, and kept by the intervenee. I find short "I" statements to be better heard and to reach their goal. "I need a moment; I love or care for you because.... I saw when you (name an incident) on (date). I felt (a feeling of concern) when I saw you (the above), and I need help with my concern." These are five short "I" statements. The more you say does less good. And a direct, loving, rehearsed group presentation can do more good with the shortest, fewest words.

Chapter 10

Interruptions

First Interruption: Anger Attack

When you conduct the maxi-intervention, Addie will probably express anger at all of you for coming together. He may say: "I can't believe you all ganged up on me like this. Why did you bring all these folks into this? This is none of that guy's business. If you cared for me one bit, why did you hurt me like this? You make me angry, ganging up on me like this!"

The interventionist will help pick the "anger man." The anger man is the most calm and possibly detached from the pain—maybe a brother-in-law, a neighbor, or a church member who is less emotionally involved and able to calmly deal with the anger man script. This same person makes a good driver or companion to escort to treatment. This assigned man or woman will quickly interrupt his anger attack interruption with a prepared written script. Maybe something like this: "Naturally, Addie, we all knew before coming here this would anger you. Wait, wait, let me finish. You may hate us the rest of our lives for being here today and revealing our feelings to one another. We agreed to risk your displeasure because we care for you that much. Now let (current reader's name) finish what she was reading to us."

The one person who approached Addie with the mini-intervention would be the best one to play the following card and saying, "We all discussed the likelihood of this gathering upsetting you. I tried to come to you one-on-one, remember, a week ago. At that time I said I would be back if there appeared to be any other way to get help for my worry. Well, I'm back with these concerned loved ones to share our collective fears and hope. Please hear us out for just a few moments.

The group hopes to finish the maxi-intervention with the happy person going off to willingly accept treatment at the proper level of care. Not likely. We will perhaps overly prepare for interruptions. I'm always amazed at how standard or universal we humans react. When confronted, he will most likely try to derail the group with a trash attack.

Second Interruption: a Trash Attack

The anger man kicks the process back on track and avoids derailing it onto anger attacks. I call the second typical interruption a "trash attack". This comes almost always aimed at one of the females in the group, usually a wife or daughter of one of the men in the group. Apparently, he wants to get someone to defend the one he verbally trashed. This takes the heat off him and stirs a discussion of the one trashed.

A typical attack might go like this: "Wait just one minute! You think I got a problem? Why aren't you jumping on this slut here's case? Why, just let me tell you all what I heard she did in 1989…"

The interventionist will also help the group select the "trash man." The husband, father, or brother of the trashed female must button his lips and just sit on it. He is obviously trying to derail the group into defending the trashed one. The assigned trash man is the one least likely to rise to defend the trashed one. He or she will surprise the interruption of trash talk by quickly reading his own interruption. This, again, could be a neighbor or friend. He might respond with, "Surely, Addie, you know us each one very well. You know every one of us here has issues and problems. We've already discussed this. Now let me finish… We all have problems. We promise we will hear and discuss any issue you have with any one of us at length later, but now, let's let (interrupted one) finish what she was saying now. Go ahead (name)."

The twelve "I" statements are finished with the above interruptions. The group expects these interruptions and has a calm rehearsed answer for each.

This trash attack happens at almost every intervention. Oddly, I've never heard of the addict or troubled person bringing up their trash attack later. This verifies that this was only a diversion to get us off track. The participants probably would be willing to discuss some family issue at length later, in a counselor-guided family session. This could be part of the family follow-up or his step work in recovery. He may think you are willing to discuss all issues today, but the group really means later. Again, this was a diverging tactic, and I do not recall ever needing to return to some trash attack issue, even in aftercare.

I once helped with a wealthy man's intervention. He had recently paid for a lavish wedding for his daughter, his "daddy's girl." But he disgusted hundreds of friends and family members with drunken behavior at the wedding and said, "Wait just a minute, let me tell you what that little slut did before marrying this bozo." His trash attack at his intervention was to begin to verbally attack the bride, his daughter. He would've even broken up his daughter's marriage just to get the group off his case. Thankfully his wife, son, and the groom stayed silent and let the rehearsed neighbor cite the prepared trash statement to put us back on track.

When the six or more witnesses finish their twelve caring, concerned statements, the closer, typically the interventionist, will make the opening offer. Again, this part probably will be interrupted with the anger and trash diversions. The opening offer goes like this: "Because these loved ones care so much for you and are hurting so much, we want you to go now with (name) in her car to (prearranged program of help). Will you go with them now?" His first answer most likely will be, "No way!"

The interventionist will urge him to accept the prearranged treatment or placement; saying, "This is an outpouring of care and concern for you. These loved ones researched the very best available level of care for you. This group agreed to ask you to join them in recovery from all this pain by going with (name of driver). We want you to go now to begin the process of recovery at the best facility."

The driver will need to stay focused and not go back over the details as the two of them travel to treatment.

A long time ago, I helped a family in far South Dallas. The lady agreed to go with the family to enter treatment. She said, "Let us all go together in my van. Then and only then will I go." Big mistake! The whole family followed me to the preselected hospital. I looked back and the big van was tilting and weaving. The family was in a big fight and rehashing all the details. The hospital worked with the family for several hours, but late that Sunday night she still refused to sign admission papers and the family took her back home in defeat. She died the next year, never trying for help again. This is one example of why only one strong person should escort the loved one into treatment.

Salesmen sometimes close a deal. The good ones quickly leave with the order. The poor salesman stays and talks more after the "yes" and loses the sale. The customer decides to think it over and maybe buy another day. This is called "selling the deal and then buying it back." We had an old salesman friend we called "Starvin' Marvin," who kept talking until the deal was closed, then reopened, and then closed, again, as in "no deal."

The spokesman or interventionist asks Addie to join the group in getting help for the collective pain. Everyone must stay silent now. A long silent period is helpful at this point. The old salesman's rule applies; the first one to speak loses. I've talked to many recovering folks after an intervention. His mind is racing at this point in the intervention, thinking, "How can I get out of this?"

Watch and pray that he says yes. Sometimes just the slightest nod or tear will signify his acceptance of help. I saw an elderly lady reluctant to accept help from her gathered loved ones at her mountain cabin. She brought her two big dogs in to pet and comfort her. She said she would never go with them and could not admit she needed their help. After about forty-five minutes of prepared scripts, there was just the slightest nod of her long-billed cap. We took this as a yes and quickly loved her into the car and rehabilitation. Checking back, she is still celebrating her recovery.

I remember an older gentleman in North Texas who came in the back door, petting his puppy. We could see him hanging on to the dog as we talked. He had a western hat down over his eyes. Finally, there was just a little nod of the hat. He began to weep with his daughters and entered treatment.

When you see the nod, quickly stand, thank him for agreeing to go, and let the escort take off with him.

Excuses

In their rehearsal sessions the group can very accurately rank his top five excuses for not joining them in the proposed program. Five members have a written script dealing with each of his top five excuses. See the sheet in the back to prepare this list.

The conversation would go like this:

Interventionist: "In light of all this outpouring of concern, is there something blocking you from joining them in seeking help for this pain?"

Intervenee: "Yes, I can't go with them because of (money or whatever the family predicted would be his first excuse)."

Assigned loved one: "Of course, we knew this would block you from going. We worked on this for some time. Our part in taking care of this will be to (help pay, secured insurance, or --). We took care of that.

Interventionist: "OK, then we can go to get help; they took care of that road block for you already."

Intervenee: "No, Way, I told you I will not go".

Interventionist: "Is there something else keeping you?"

Intervenee: "I cannot go because (second excuse)".

Second assigned loved one: "Here is how we handled that for you…"

Interventionist: "Will you go?" The room needs to be silent a long time. There comes a time when the first to speak loses. Eighty percent of the time he will angrily get up and say, "Let's go".

Most likely he will at first refuse to accept the proposed treatment. I've never seen anyone offer more than five reasons or excuses for not accepting help. I am amazed at how accurately the family group can predict his excuses and even rank the order from first to last.

"No way! I'm not going to any treatment place."

The interventionist will try to extract from him some of the five rehearsed excuses the group predicted would come out.

"I can't go. I have no one to care for the kids."

The assigned one will say, "Of course, we talked about this problem; that is why Mom and I took off work this week to stay with the kids for you. Our part will be to take care of them, while your part is to go get help."

The interventionist says, "Then it's taken care of. Let's go now."

Addie may say: "I told you; I'm flat not going."

The interventionist replies: "Will you tell us what else could block you from going?"

The loved ones may know he will mention his sinking boat at the lake next. A cousin answered "Sure! I knew you could not go anywhere with that boat leaking at the lake. That is why I borrowed a big boat trailer, and I am going to get the boat out of the lake today while you go get help. I promise to work with you to patch your boat so we can fish again like we used to, after you come home."

Eliciting and dealing with each excuse calmly and in order leads him to acceptance. Do not panic if he is resisting with excuses. This is precisely the step the group expected and rehearsed. His excuses are part of the process, one of the main parts of the dance. He may indicate he could go if only this hurdle could be overcome. The group does not minimize his logic, but it has already studied this problem in depth and formulated the best solution so he can have treatment.

Dismiss Addie

If he still says "NO WAY!" then the group has said all they can say. This took about thirty minutes, no more than forty minutes. Excuse him from the session at this point. The interventionist should say, "Thank you for hearing us out. That is all we have to say at this time. You are excused to leave now. This group is disappointed and sad. After all has been said, he may choose to not accept the offer of help. When the interventionist determines he is absolutely not going to treatment, the group has said all they can. Do not repeat the pleas.

The interventionist will then bluntly say, "Thank you for listening. This is all we are saying to you today. We are pledged to remain in this room (or down the road at another meeting place) for forty-five more minutes. We plan to discuss further commitments and support for one another during the next forty-five minutes. It is nine fifteen. We will be here (or there) until ten. If you reconsider helping us with this plan, come back or call the cell phone number before ten. Again, thank you for listening. Please leave now." No hugs; just let him walk out.

Reinforce the Pledges of Change

Most families shudder at putting him out of the session alone. But no one should follow him out for a private one-on-one discussion. He needs to feel total isolation. His loved ones are together discussing commitments. What does *commitment* mean? He might wonder if the group is discussing some court action such as an involuntary mental health commitment.

The group will be in grief. The family would benefit from a few family counseling sessions after an intervention, whether the intervention was successful or not. Often he will call to discuss his options and agree to find help this day or soon. The family needs to feel assured they did all they could at any point in the dance.

Suicide Fears

Typically, when I meet with concerned others regarding change, confrontation, setting new boundaries, and consequences, the question of suicide comes up: "What if we confront him, and offer consequences if he doesn't seek help, and then he leaves the meeting and kills himself?" This is a possibility. I cannot promise he will not do this. After helping with well over 800 organized interventions, I have seen no one commit suicide yet. I believe suicide comes from a lack of hope, no choice but to die. An intervention offers a solution, a plan of action, joining together with loved ones to get help for the pain. This is why we intervene and offer hope. The group gives him an avenue of hope and help and urges him to accept hope.

When we exercise this last option of having him leave the group, almost every addict comes back in the forty-five minute time and reluctantly agrees to go to treatment. Should he not come back, we would reinforce our pledge of ceasing all cover-ups and enabling. Urge Al-Anon support group attendance, stay in touch, and protect any vulnerable person from danger or reprisals from this effort. Keep phone numbers of the group and the treatment facility. He will most likely call or visit the weakest link to get more information or reengage them in enabling behaviors. Sadly I see some go back, hang back as we leave, and offer him comfort and a promise to come back later to enable his historically damaging behavior.

Stay in touch with the group and maintain solidarity. If he calls you for help, quickly rearrange the desired transportation and admission. If he calls ask: "Are you ready for help? If not, get back to me whenever you are ready. Good-bye until then."

Well prepared interventions succeed to admission 90 percent of the time.

Chapter 11

Roadblocks to Success and Serenity

Here are twenty-five roadblock excuses for why recovery won't be successful and my responses:

1. "He must bottom out before he is ready to accept help or even allow an effective offer of help." We will show this to be a myth.

2. "The loved one, spouse, mother, father, etc., drove him to do it." No way!

3. "He is too old to change; we should have done something years ago." Some of the strongest recoveries occur with older people.

4. "Our family cannot confront, he is a very private person." Reading this book will help confront.

5. "For religious reasons, we cannot confront!" I love it when a member of the group says, "We cannot do this because we are believers, and believers must turn the other cheek, serve, go the extra mile, etc."

    The Good Teacher, Jesus, taught, loosely paraphrased here, to go to someone with a problem one on one. If that does not get results, take someone with you. If that fails, take him to a group of believers. If that fails, in order to retrieve him, there will be serious consequences. So, I don't feel disobedient when

I help organize a loving confrontation. I would suggest that they recall the instances when two or three have asked him to find help. Is the next step of the dance to take him to a group of believers?

6. "There is no money to provide treatment." My training and efforts are to help find viable available appropriate help. Many organizations offer resources for folks seeking assistance. The most effective interventions I've seen were without money for treatment.

   I remember a dad taking his son to the parking lot of a convenience store. He gave him six dollars in quarters. He gave him a paper with three names and phone numbers. He said he knew someone would come and give him a ride to one of these three programs. They were (1) the Salvation Army for "two hots and a cot" with a treatment program available upon request; (2) the Presbyterian Night Shelter, near bus lines, for jobs; and (3) the Union Gospel Mission. (There are similar facilities in many cities). He read his son the note telling him to "never give out the home address as his again. This will never be your home or address again." The young man stayed at the Union Gospel Mission, and was promoted to store manager at a small convenience store.

   I've known three friends who went into a two-year program where they worked for their own payment. Two out of the three went on to become helpers of other folks with needs. Counties have treatment programs available. Some have requirements of a waiting list or to get there early on Monday mornings to weed out those who do not have a sincere desire. Plenty of help is available without money. Of course, paid programs usually have more staff, and arrangements can be made for check-in even before you intervene. Having a firm place ready to check in makes an intervention easier and helps with success.

7. "He will not ever go with us, no matter what we do." That is his choice. We will be satisfied we did do all we could to offer a good choice. A widow knows she did all she could for a terminally ill spouse. There comes a point in time to accept the reality you have absolutely done all you can do.

8. "His spouse uses also and will cause him to relapse." After he begins recovery, he will accept his responsibility to maintain recovery and learn healthy boundaries with all loved ones and acquaintances. "

   "He will only relapse." Possibly so. In some cases a relapse is good in bringing the reality that he really does have a serious problem. We accept that he does have another relapse left in him; he just may not have another recovery experience left in him.

   "He tried once before and failed." Many in successful recovery failed in early attempts to achieve abstinence.

9. "He will be angry and hate us." the concerned others stated to him. "Because we care enough for you; even if you hate all of us for the rest of your life, we are willing to accept that risk."

10. "He will tell others of our issues." We said to him, "You know us well; we all have issues. We are willing to discuss any issue you know about any one of us at length, *later*." Any discussion will be held in a therapeutic, safe environment, with proper professional assistance on hand. There we can discuss any issue or accusations.

11. "He will not follow up with aftercare." We pointed out choices and consequences. He is completely responsible for his choices.

12. "His family will give in and start enabling again." The family and acquaintances will try to continue confronting past patterns of enabling. Counselors love the opportunity to do family sessions with a group after an intervention.

13. "There is no support group available for him." Support groups of one sort or another are always available, even in the smallest of communities. National Internet addresses, the local ministries, even the police department can put you in touch with support groups. In the Dallas / Fort Worth area, someone counted 176 individual AA or NA groups per day to serve—morning groups, lunch groups, and evening groups.

14. "It is normal to use at his work or school." He is still completely responsible for his behavior.

15. "He has to have his pain medication to survive." Treatment professionals can help find appropriate pain management.

16. "His medical doctor pushes him to medicate." Some doctors are guilty of overmedication. We see celebrities with their personal doctors being charged with enabling. We still intervene and help see the irrational use of these doctors. I find most medical doctors are helping reduce pain and discomfort, whatever it takes. Some doctors are building a practice, not trying to run folks off from coming back to receive help. The doctors realize if they confront a patient regarding addiction, the patient will simply not come back to that office. Experienced prescription addicts profile various medical offices to approach for writing a "script." An addict prefers a free-standing single doctor practice outside a large city where they can keep talking about reactions from previous medication until the doctor writes the script of choice. Some great doctors will help with an intervention for their addicted patient.

17. "He has to go to court so cannot go to rehab." Rehabilitation will enhance his court case. Some attorneys would prefer to be able to say to the court, "My client is unable to appear because he is an in-patient at a hospital. May we have a postponement?" When the time comes for a court date, it is good to be able to report to the judge with proof of successful treatment, proof of daily attendance of support group meetings, and a written report from a testing lab of drug- and alcohol-free testing over several months. These are sometimes requirements ordered by

a judge. Reporting a completion of what the judge wants to see may entice the judge to give probation or time served instead of jail time. This saves the court and taxpayers a lot of money and obviously is in the best interest of the entire family system. When anyone says we cannot intervene because of a pending court appearance, I say, "Ask the attorney." Hopefully, the attorney will encourage a confrontation or intervention to aid the prospect of a better outcome.

I remember a client in my office shaking and sweating profusely. Her family insisted on her coming to a counseling session with me instead of confronting her as a family. She needed a drug fix immediately and was in severe withdrawals. She was going before the judge the next day to receive a probation arranged by her family to avoid jail time. I begged her to go to a medical detoxification program available to her. She insisted on getting a fix instead so she could give a good appearance to the judge. She got an extended probation and did not have to see her new probation officer for some time. Before her probation officer appointment she overdosed and died. I grieved her death with the family.

18. "No interventionist is available to help us." The caring group can very well conduct an intervention using this book and other sources, along with telephone encouragement.

19. "No one else knows of his issue." If two or three discuss this problem, most often they discover a neighbor, fellow worker, ex-spouse, a child, or some angry person caring enough to help.

20. "No one will help with an intervention." Ask the question, "Do you think I need to be concerned about his well-being?" If "perhaps" then say, "Would you meet to discuss possible approaches to assist him?"

21. "No one ever asked him one-on-one." Then use the mini-intervention for a five-minute one-on-one intervention.

22. "He will sue us or cause legal issues." He could, but we are not using accusing language, but simply stating personal eyewitness situations and how we are affected. Then we ask for help with our burden. If we furnish a forum for liable accusations, hearsay, or damaging information, we are wronging him. We are not doing anything most lawyers could find cause to take his case.

23. "He will not begin treatment or recovery because all his buddies are doing the same behavior." It's still his responsibility. I've done a few interventions with buddies assisting while hiding or even admitting their own problems. A few times the intervention brought the buddy or brother to recognize he was doing the same to his own family, and he also sought help for his issues.

    We are not going to include or discuss confronting anyone with another person having a serious issue such as a housemate or significant other who is using heavily with him. We cannot succeed in an intervention to convince two buddies to accept change at the same meeting. We intend to introduce him to new buddies who are clean and sober.

24. "Even if he goes into treatment, he will not stay."

    Let's give the professionals and the group dynamics an opportunity to work their magic.

25. "His friends will simply check him out of treatment."

    There is an advantage to using a treatment program away from town. This gives more gravity to the program, being some distance from home. The main advantage is that his using buddies will be less likely to visit, to encourage him from leaving the program AMA (against medical advice). The disadvantages of a far-away program is the difficulty of family and significant others joining in family therapy sessions and in the client's participation in partial or day programming and in aftercare sessions provided by the treatment facility.

Chapter 12

Legal Fears

Some people fear being sued for attacking or spreading damaging information beyond the circle of loved ones. You are *not* going to use any person who is clearly quoting hearsay or gossip regarding Addie. These six or more willing participants will be stating significant incidents they've personally seen or heard. They will *not* use statements such as "You are always doing…" or "You never…" Instead, you will be reading statements like "On a Thursday night last November, I answered the hall telephone. Addie, you called with very slurred speech and cursed your mom by calling her an xxx." If a participant cannot say the words or reveals real pain because they want to protect Addie, then I might consider this as enabling behavior from one of Addie's support system.

Regarding legal concerns, in the 1990s some interventionists, mental health professionals, and treatment facilities got a black eye from using unethical practices in Texas. Several went to prison, lost their livelihood, or paid hefty fines after investigations of various forms of interventions were reported. Unscrupulous people trolled Alcoholic Anonymous meetings and other support groups to find and net possible admissions to hospitals and treatment programs. Hospitals received offers from these trollers to bring in up to five admissions at a time for a finder's fee of one thousand dollars a head. These trollers became known as "head hunters." Some treatment center administrators encouraged and/

or turned a blind eye to this fiercely competitive marketing approach. Hospitals belonging to the same chain fought each other for ranking and survival. It is clearly unethical for an interventionist to harvest or market hurting bodies for one particular treatment option.

Part of the cleanup involved the closure of many treatment programs, investigations, filed legal charges, and ordered consequences. A major improvement, and an advantage to licensed professionals, is the requirement for an interventionist to have a state license. This helped curtail the wholesale profitability of marketing to hurting families.

I was very fortunate through those years to work for a facility that directed me to help families acquire treatment wherever they found it available. For several years I facilitated twenty to twenty-five family interventions per month. Now I do three to five per month with a 90 percent success rate of agreement to accept the proposed level of care.

The main reason for a high rate of success is my lack of coercion of any of the proposed participants. If one wants to back out at even the last minute, this is okay. If I don't feel we have compelling information that pushes us to carry through with the intervention, then I am the first to abort the current attempt. Perhaps we could gather more evidence, get other participants with stronger statements, or use an alternative approach. When we rehearse the successful intervention, we will always know we must try to assist the hurting one to accept some form of therapy. If anyone does not feel a strong urge to carry through, then they can and must drop out.

I read two depositions of lawsuits where the intervenee sued the interventionist, his employer, and his family members. In a Southern state, a lawyer sued his colleagues for bringing in participants that could hurt him. In Texas, a hospital group brought in upper management who had no firsthand information to urge the employee to seek help. She did go away to treatment but came back to sue the group and the hospital.

The cases included using participants who cited hearsay statements such as, "Someone told me they saw you drinking too much. You are an alcoholic. You always make me angry."

I refuse to attend a meeting with anyone without hearing his or her own written eyewitness accounts. I will not allow judgmental statements or "You make me angry" statements. I do not want to be part of an attack or a lawsuit. I insist on involving only firsthand witnesses of some inappropriate behavior.

I remember a brother once who refused to write down what he intended neither to say nor to tell the group what he would say. He wanted to just "shoot from the hip, speak from his heart, to say what he meant." I refused to go with this group from fear of libelous or out of control, dangerous, harmful statements.

I remember meeting with a group of concerned folks to consider trying to get a dad to seek help for his apparent drinking problem. His nine-year-old daughter wanted to read this note she had written: "Daddy, I love you. I am your daddy's girl. Three weeks ago I brought four friends into the living room after school. We saw some beer bottles on the coffee table. You were in your underwear. Daddy, you staggered around and you peed on our couch with my girlfriends running out of the room. Daddy, I felt so embarrassed, scared, and angry at you. Daddy, please help me with my fear by going with us to get help."

The grandmother, Daddy's mom, interrupted, shouting that we could not use this note; it was way too disgusting to hear in front of these friends. We talked again of the long history of some of the group letting things go by and covering awkward moments. Most of the group was aware they wanted to stop being part of the problem by suffering the consequences of his drinking episodes. When they were hurting the most, he was feeling little or no pain because he was typically out of it. He may have felt awful later, but at the time, he was perhaps attempting to self-medicate all his uncomfortable feelings. The group finally agreed to let the daughter read her incident to her dad on the morning of the intervention. The dad refused to go with the group to start recovery.

Later, the little girl read her written consequence statement: "Daddy, I'm just nine years old and can't make you do anything. All I can do is promise you I can never bring a friend to our home unless you get help." Well, we all cried when he got up, hugged his kid and went off to a treatment center with his brother.

It took the strong, brave statements from the daughter to start the process, or the dance, to attain recovery. Again, to spare the pain by hiding an incident could be enabling the continuing behavior.

This story illustrates why I am aware of legal issues but believe a properly conducted intervention is effective when other approaches have failed.

Chapter 13

Intervention Participants

You must eventually have at least six willing witnesses of Addie's disturbing behaviors to carry off a successful maxi-intervention. You are not ordering them to come. You are simply asking if they are concerned and could gather to evaluate these suggestions in order to offer help.

These six or more folks may be neighbors, church or social acquaintances, fellow workers, ex-spouses, etc.

Good Witnesses

I conduct interventions with two and once even with three ex-spouses attending the session. The three ex-wives were sitting on a couch together when he came in. He asked, "What in the #0X#0 are you three doing together?" The oldest ex-wife read her script, "We are all here because we care for your well-being. Please sit down as we ask you to hear about something very important to all of us." Addie's first impression may be that the group is about to tell him of some family tragedy. You will quickly get to the issue and not play on this fear of a family tragedy. However, his ongoing problem without attention is a looming tragedy for this family or group of concerned others.

I have a very good memory of a young man twenty-three years old. His parents remarried when he was very young and they had no personal contact for many years. When he arrived, his biological parents were sitting together. Both stepparents were there. His mom said, "Please sit down and listen to all your parents, because we all love you." Everyone in the room cried as he went with his dad and stepfather to check into a drug treatment center. He has since helped me conduct two interventions for a couple of buddies. An old cliché from support groups is, "You can't keep it unless you give it away." This young man is working the twelfth step of his twelve-step recovery program, using the learned principals to help others.

Children

Children eight years old or more can be awesome as intervention participants. Many folks are reluctant to involve children in such an emotional meeting. But a child psychiatrist helped me see the probable lack of harm to children. If children are a firsthand witness of extreme inappropriate behavior, they are already hurting. Two possibilities are available.

First, if the intervention fails and the family member refuses help, the child can remember the family tried its best and the child did all he could to help at the time. The child needs some validation to realize the care and concern and the reality that he was honored and allowed to try to help. The child will someday recall these caring efforts by concerned others.

Second, if the loved one accepts help and celebrates recovery, the child will be a part of the success and will recall an act of love that brought intimacy to the family. Either way, the child can know the family did make a good effort.

Out-of-Towners

The best participants are a significant person, grandparent, uncle, aunt, past church leader, or teacher who comes in as a surprise from out of town because they care that much. It's more moving and impressive than merely using local participants.

If a significant person wants to be present but is not able to attend, a small tape recorder or cell phone on speaker with a similar message cued up to play at the exact best time can serve as one of the six needed participants. The recorded message may go like this: "I wish I could be with you there. I care for you. I saw you [tell incident] and felt express feelings]. I sure hope you join our loved ones there in getting some relief for my feeling of... Bye." This tape in the midst of other statements can be emotionally moving. But a recorded conversation, even on a cell's speaker phone, is not as good as in-person statements.

Some folks discuss having a loved one phone in their statement during the intervention. This is a bad idea. You would lose control of when in the process this call might come in. You also lose control of the conversation.

Divide and Conquer

So often Addie will urge one person to go outside to smoke and/or work it all out one-on-one, away from the group. Addie will take a brother outside; you may hear talking, shouts, crying, and you may think progress is happening. Then you will most likely hear Addie driving off and the brother who went outside with him will come in and say, "Addie is never going to treatment." I allowed that to happen a long time ago, but never again. We just blew all our cards and lost the opportunity to use the power of the group dynamic. The appropriate answer is, "Sure Bud, I will discuss anything you want to talk about at great length, *later*. Just let us wrap up in here first."

In other words, do not let him split up the group.

Difficult Siblings

A proposed intervention is at risk when Addie has an older sister involved. I do not remember an older sister organizing an intervention for her brother. Typically, a sister sometimes sabotages a strong attempt to confront her brother, especially if he is a younger brother. An older sister may remember taking part in raising her younger brother. If the group wants to imply he has a problem, this reflects on her parenting skills for him.

I remember planning an intervention for a certified public accountant who had an older sister who helped raise him. He hit his wife and hurt their children when he drank. Their home had holes in the wall from shoving a child and from throwing objects. Relatives came in from over a thousand miles away to help confront him and urge him to enter treatment. His wife's brother is a lawyer and was ready to share his well-written script at the correct time. We gathered for the final rehearsal on a Saturday evening. I felt we had plenty of documentation to break through his denial or his delusion that he did not have a problem.

His brother-in-law led us in a prayer for divine intervention and guidance for success the next morning. His older sister had flown in from New England to see that he received the best of care. She stood and started screeching, berating, yelling at all of us. She said this would hurt her brother, and he did not deserve to be confronted. She said if we thought he had a problem, she took this as a personal attack on her, since she partially raised him. Her brother would not be available for an intervention the next morning or ever. She had already told him the words of our scripts and bought him a flight to New Orleans. She was so upset with her parents and all of us that she fell down in the floor. I may have imagined it, but I even saw foam on her mouth.

The lawyer, brother of the wife, calmly brought out the legal restraining order papers he said he hoped and prayed not to use. He also verified the report to Child Protection Services. He said he and his family would not let his sister stay in the home and suffer any chance of future abuse. He had prearranged alternative housing for his sister, nieces, and nephew to stay in that night and had a long-range plan of safety. He told the addict's sister that she had sabotaged the last effort to save her brother. I've witnessed this similar dynamic more than once. I urge you not to include a protective-older-sister type helper too early in the process.

Joint Interventions

Do not try to conduct a joint intervention with two possible substance using or troubled folks at the same time. They will stick together in not agreeing for either to seek recovery.

A brother or friend who uses chemicals or is involved heavily in the behavior you wish to confront will sabotage your efforts. Do not include a "using" spouse or someone with a similar compulsive behavior in your intervention. A spouse involved in the same activity absolutely will abort your attempt to get help. Do *not* inform these parties of any pending exercise seeking treatment or placement in a recovery program. You can intervene with the second one separately and later.

I once helped with three interventions the same rainy night. Two sisters and one of their husbands were drugging heavily together. A large group confronted them one at a time. A different driver took the first two individually to separate treatment facilities. By the time we got to the third family member we were reduced in number of concerned family members to escort him to the third prearranged hospital. He did enter treatment that night, but at last report he had relapsed while his wife and sister-in-law remain in abstinence.

The concerned others prepared with individually written scripts from intervention scripts. Each had two written reasons why they cared for the intervenee, two specific witnessed incidents, and what they pledged to change, even if no one else changes their behavior.

A unified effort magnifies the success of an intervention. It has been wisely said, "Uniformity is absolutely impossible in human enterprise. Unity is absolutely essential on human enterprise."

You and/or others may have tried to approach an addicted person in the past to no avail. Addie either does not realize there is any problem or is refusing to seek viable, available, appropriate solutions. Ask questions to learn if an intervention is the best approach or learn of other approaches.

Chapter 14

Mini-interventions

Why discuss mini-interventions last when it really is conducted before a maxi-intervention?

A mini-intervention succeeds 20 percent of the time. This approach is especially effective when a loved one comes in from out of town and surprises the subject with the importance of concern. And that concerned person's going back home immediately after conducting a mini-intervention is advised. It shows she did not come to town on other business and casually brought up a concern, but instead she traveled all that way only to try to get agreement of accepting help.

We once prepared to conduct a maxi-intervention with a middle-aged man with a drinking problem. His uncle accepted the assignment to try a mini-intervention. Uncle Max flew in from California, rented a car, and drove out to the West Texas business of his nephew.

He said: "I need five minutes. I love you because you are my hunting buddy, Nephew. While hunting last November you were drinking and shot a hole in my tent. I feel scared for our safety. Will you go with me to Red Oaks Center today to get an opinion regarding my fears?"

His nephew said, "No way."

Uncle Max said, "Get back with me if you change your mind. If I think of a better way to approach you, I will be back". He left.

Nephew asked, "Where are you going"?

Uncle Max said, "I have a return flight home to California. I came here not to visit but to simply ask you to go with me for help. If there is a better plan, I'll get back to you."

The next week I helped the guy enter a treatment center group two counties away. He told the above story and how impressed he was to see his uncle so concerned and come so far, make his point and abruptly leave. I never told him he had not checked in to the hospital his family had already prearranged. Nor did I ever tell him of coaching his uncle or having helped rehearse Uncle Max's little mini-intervention. We never needed to do the prepared maxi-intervention.

Doing the mini-intervention correctly will buy the concerned others a permit to conduct the maxi-intervention as needed. It offers a license to approach him with a group because he declined to listen to the one who came alone.

If the subject were to ask, "Why did you gang up on me? If you thought I needed help, why did you not come alone?" Uncle Max would have said, "I did come two weeks ago, but you said, 'No way!' I told you then I might be back with a better plan. And I'm back with these five others now."

MINI-INTERVENTION SCRIPTS AND AN UNWILLING LISTENER

Set the scene: A calm, private, across-the-kitchen-table, Sunday-morning, hands-on-hand scenario.

A written script on the back of a card should include the five points listed below, contingency sentences for anger and trash answers, and a plan to close the talk and walk away. Use no labels, no opinions, and no judgments such as "You always," "You never," or "You ___ too much." Instead use only "I" statements.

MINI-INTERVENTION SCRIPT WORKSHEET

Five Statements to Begin

1. "Please hear me out, I need just five minutes to say something very important to me."

2. "I love (care for / admire / respect) you because .... (short statement)."

3. "I remember seeing or hearing you... (recall a specific time and place of a painful behavior)."

4. "Seeing or hearing that, I felt... (insert one true feeling word)."

5. "I hope you will join me today in seeking a second opinion / options / choices for my discomfort." (Have a proposed appointment or help prearranged at the earliest moment.)

Contingency Statements

If Addie interrupts with an anger statement, quickly interrupt and read:

"Sure, I was afraid this would upset you. I accepted the risk because I care for you so much. Now, please, let me finish. I only asked for five minutes."

If a trash statement comes out such as, "What about your sorry mother? I know some trash about her!"

Then you quickly interrupt with, "Of course, you know us all well. We all have some issues. I pledged before starting this to discuss any issue you might have at length later. Now please, let me finish. I only asked for five minutes."

He will probably answer, "No way! I'm not going to discuss this problem with anyone."

At that point, immediately leave the table to do some preplanned activity, saying over your shoulder, "Thank you for hearing me. If you change your mind or think of a different solution to my pain, then get back with me. If I think of a better approach, I will get back to you later."

Then walk away, get coffee, read the paper, etc. You have said clearly you care, presented an option, and put the ball of responsibility clearly in his court. Leave it alone for at least a week or ten days.

The next step may be a group, well-rehearsed maxi-intervention conducted by a professional.

A Five-Minute Maximum

A mini-intervention must last no more than five minutes and must be one-on-one. Do *not* do a mini-intervention with two or more concerned others if there is any possibility of conducting a maxi-intervention later. This effort must be done only one-on-one. You will be playing too many cards that you cannot use later. A mini-intervention is simply a setup for a potential maxi-intervention at a later date.

Chapter 15

After Agreeing to Accept Help

Addie agrees to accept treatment. So now what?

The Trip to Treatment

Do not allow the large group to go with the driver to treatment admission. Preferably a single driver / escort will go with him to check in. Sometimes this involves an airplane trip; at other times it's by car.

Who Goes with Him to Treatment?

The accompanying person must be the strongest emotional person available. Do not go over the statements or rehash the event. If Addie is just silent on the way to treatment, this will be easier. Often he will be thinking of reasons or ways to back out of accepting help. If several are accompanying him to therapy, then the forum is still in session and he can start up the discussion of going or not.

The car to go to the airport or treatment is ready, car seating arrangement decided, and one, or a maximum of only two people, assigned to accompany the intervenee.

I told earlier of a successful intervention failing when too many loved ones continued to discuss the plans on the way to treatment. An argument broke out in the vanload of people, and since that meant there was no closure on the decision to accept treatment, the deal was off. I went to the hospital to mediate the family feud that was ongoing in the admission office. When only one or two people escort Addie to treatment, they need to assume the deal is decided and not rehash the decision. They are in real danger of buying the deal back, as many salesmen do when they keep talking past a yes. If there is a discussion of backing out on the way, these two can say, "What will I tell your (mom) after her tears of joy if you promised to seek help and now you don't follow up? She'll be brokenhearted. You'll need to tell her what caused you to go back on your word."

Another person reneged when the escorts stopped on the way to buy gasoline. One group I followed to the treatment center turned around to go back to the house to leave some keys. Once you get to a yes, keep going until the mission is finished, which is to check in to the viable, appropriate, available level of help and care.

If he insists on jumping out of the escort's car, the escort will pull over and let him out. The escort will not enable him to back out by taking him home. If he is silent all the way, then silence is good. The escort will not babble on to reinforce the decision. If he is suffering withdrawals, a medical risk, say from lack of alcohol on a longer trip, the escort may need to buy him a bottle or a drink on the airplane to avoid risk and to arrive at the detox center safely, even if drunk.

In the 1970s my job was to do interventions and sometimes drive a patient to the hospital. A few times I feared my patient was going into a seizure, so I stopped and bought him a cheap bottle of wine to avoid a medical emergency. He was going into a medical detoxification treatment anyway, so arriving a little more toxic but alive was okay.

Be Prepared

The escort knows the route and arrangements, not stopping for directions. Any delays will tell Addie that the group was not prepared and never expected that he might really go off to accept treatment. This intervention will be a highly practiced maneuver with full expectations of success. This will breed confidence in Addie. The facility is expecting his admission and will welcome him warmly into the assessment and admission process. The escort will exit as quickly as possible from the treatment facility, leaving the staff to bond with him.

Chapter 16

Early Days of Treatment

My office in a treatment hospital was near the pay telephone. Many times I overheard a new patient making calls begging a sister, mom, wife, or drugging friend to please come and check him out of this bad place. I heard: "Come get me! This is a mean place! The night nurse is horrible, the counselor (me) is a jerk, the food is cold, the bed is hard, nothing but street bums are in here! I don't belong here!"

Oddly, every inpatient knows and continually tells one another of the laws that say if you request to leave, you can leave. When someone did come and check them out of the hospital AMA (against medical advice) the patient would normally say, "See there, my friend agreed I did not belong here and is taking me home." On those occasions, more than one patient would leave. One left with the family that came to pick up their patient early, and then another patient wanted to leave early also.

So please do not enable your loved one to continue the destructive behavior by helping anyone to check out early. They can have the courage to check themselves out but usually will not. They want to put the responsibility on you, and the family to blame you, for folding on perhaps their last chance for a recovering life style. Some insurance companies refuse to pay for treatment when the patient checks out early—AMA. Thus, the patient or family that signed him in can become liable for paying for treatment that did little or no good. But sometimes a patient saying they do not need a program does come to an awakening when they go out and return to the failing system as their life was before. So a good relapse can become a key part of a long-term recovery. Everyone has another potential binge behavior left in them. They may not have another chance for recovery or detoxification left in them at some point.

Early Reluctance after Admission

Other licensed professionals in the treatment field have discussed many times the reluctance of everyone in early recovery. We do not remember any clients or patients truly having an awakening and suddenly deciding to check into treatment on their own. A common line of a recent patient admission is, "I just got sick and tired of being sick and tired, so I decided on my own to check myself into this program."

Old-timers in recovery often confront these newbies with lines such as, "Shut up! You can't B.S. a B.S.-er." Everyone I can think of was coerced into checking into a treatment program. He was facing job loss, family losses, serious health losses, legal consequences, or some other consequence of continuing to do his destructive behavior. Most patients are angry the first few days or a week of reluctantly entering a program. The 40 percent of patients who make the first 90 days of recovery are the ones who buy into the process of recovery within a week of entering the facility.

If 90 percent of interventions yield an admission, and 40 percent of admissions make successful recovery for 90 days, that means 90 multiplied by 40 equals 36 percent. If you conduct a full-blown maxi-intervention, you can reasonably expect the odds of your loved one being in recovery three months later are 36 percent. You might think these are not good enough odds. Intervention is for those we have tried everything else we can think of to gain acceptance of help for. This may be the last gasp effort for this family. If someone is diagnosed with a fatal illness and given a 36 percent chance to enter remission, most would try the recommended treatment. To me, the real hurdles to get over are ninety days, when many relapse, and the twenty-four month wall. After twenty-four months of recovery the desires are less intense, less frequent, and of shorter duration. (See "Cravings per Lifetime" in the next chapter.)

Many treatment programs offer a family week or a family Saturday for educational and bonding purposes. This activity can be the strongest component of recovery. Please make every effort to take the time to attend any and all family and friends programs. Some family members visit too much and interrupt the therapeutic setting. Go with the treatment center's guidelines. Ask questions of staff.

During and After Treatment

Going into the desired treatment is not the end of recovery. Follow up with aftercare, family members going to support groups such as Al-Anon for family meetings, relapse avoidance measures, and maintaining credibility in the areas of family changes will need to be reinforced.

Intervention is only the beginning of change.

We have zero hope of success if he does not follow up with the recommended level of aftercare. I cannot find anyone with two years of recovery post-treatment experience who did not attend support groups and use a sponsor. Some family members will become disappointed when he chooses to attend support group meetings and confer with his sponsor at the same hour of a family dinner. His recovery must take precedence, especially for the first ninety days after formal treatment.

Chapter 17

Continuing Care

It is certainly Addie's choice to leave before treatment is complete. We, as a group, point out consequences of not seeking help. I want the message clear that the group of concerned others will stick together in carrying out the consequences discussed if he leaves early or does not embrace recovery. In the ten years I worked with a chemical dependency hospital, I overheard many tearful pleas over the telephone to come check them out. I heard exaggerated complaints of bad food, bad roommates, bad staff, and bad pain without enough pain relief. It seems strange the patient can simply say, "I want to leave now."

In the absence of a life-threatening situation, the treatment facility will help him leave within a few hours. If someone comes to take him home early, He will say later; "See, my sister or my loved one knew I did not need to be in that horrible place. They came and got me out." Because the typical patient in withdrawal discomfort wants someone else to make the choice to come check him out, he usually plays on their guilt or self-examination if they even did the right thing to do this coercion to go for help. The first several days of treatment are critical and some check out early.

During the first week of treatment many patients minimize the problem and look upon their situation as minor compared to fellow patients. When families visit he may point out how much worse the other's problems are, telling family that he is forced to be in the wrong level of care. In the patient therapy group a common new comer statement goes like this, "I came to realize I was just sick and tired of being sick and tired, so I decided on my own to check in here." Typically the group dynamics kick in with a co-patient asking, What was about to happen to you if you did not come into the program"? I do not remember an in-patient who just came in without some form of loss or pain pending in the background.

Support Group

Please use the sheet below to build trust that attendance at support groups is happening. This can be free will or in submission of an agreement to claim compliance to a recovery protocol. I urge at least four support groups per week the first ninety days of abstinence of the compulsive behavior. Many groups and therapists expect ninety meetings in the first ninety days of recovery. Obviously this would be even better. Some report they would never have achieved recovery without following this "Ninety in Ninety" regimen. The concerned others, with some professional advice, might allow one or two of these support group sessions to be religious meetings or other support groups. I started using the expression "celebrating recovery" long before the very successful Celebrate Recovery program began. This is a weekly group meeting around the country begun by Saddleback Church. You can find their meeting places and material on their website.

Sponsor

Within the first two weeks of the recovery process, a named sponsor is so important. The person entering this new lifestyle of recovery would have difficulty doing this alone. The recovering person can note who is active at the support group. Instead of asking that person to become a sponsor, he or she might ask, "Will you suggest someone to be a temporary sponsor to help me get started for a couple of weeks?" If this temporary sponsor does not fit, then it is easier to thank them and move on to a second or even third sponsor for a good fit as a mentor or support source. See the "Trust Building Sign-In Sheet" in the worksheets section.

Cravings per Life Time

What if doctors tested a large number of people with a compulsive behavior? Suppose the doctors discovered the average likely number of cravings expected in the future lifetime of someone in recovery from a compulsive behavior. What if this number of cravings is 2,790 per lifetime? Twelve-step recovery groups knew a long time ago of the importance of the first ninety days of recovery. That's why the "Ninety in Ninety" regimen is a common protocol during the first ninety days of abstinence. The first ninety days of recovery are tough, but the first few days are the toughest, especially day one, so we have hope of this getting easier in time.

During the first ninety days of recovery, or of breaking through, the cravings are intense, frequent, and lengthy. The thoughts of returning to the behavior may occur twenty-two times a day. The desire, need, and obsessing on the habit is intense. So the first ninety days can help work through about 1980 of the 2,790 cravings per recovering lifetime. This leaves only 880 more to work through. The person is *almost* totally detoxified at the end of ninety days. During the first two years, the cravings can drop down to about one a day from the previous 22 a day. In two years this recovery has gotten through another 770 cravings. In two years and ninety days he is down to 40 cravings for the rest of his lifetime. Certainly these of are of shorter duration, less frequent, and less intense. He is, for all practical purposes, detoxified. That offers much hope of recovery.

However, I illustrate this with a runner. Marathon runners know of the wall somewhere after twenty miles. The carbs are burned up and the body cannot go on. Some drop out after twenty miles of a twenty-six mile run. Others are aware of this ominous runner's wall, get a second wind, and run through the finish line waving, "Hi Mom".

Check it out, so many recovering folks fall out and relapse right around ninety days. The thought is that the brain has a need to feel normal with the compulsive activity or substance. The residue is almost gone and the mind sets up situations and scenarios to get the body fixed or a get a fix. Cocaine addicts especially hit a wall at ninety days, but other recovering folks have a similar pattern. After two years and ninety days the cravings are certainly not as intense, frequent, or long lasting. The point is, if he starts over, has a slip, goes back even briefly to the old behavior, the cravings come back in a few days and he is starting over with a fresh 2,790 set of compulsions to fight. Thus, recovery is a celebration, but not a cure.

Conclusion

"I myself am convinced, my brothers, that you yourselves are full of goodness, complete in knowledge and competent to instruct one another" (Romans 15:14, NIV). These are inspired words from the apostle Paul.

You are certainly full of goodness to even read and consider helping someone who is hard to help. You and I care unconditionally for this person and can realize God sees the innate goodness in this person and in each of us.

You are full of knowledge and informed of your particular situation. You probably are the only one seeing the reality of this complete story.

You have the goodness, knowledge, freedom, and responsibility to make a smart choice this day and plan to tomorrow.

You are choosing *not* to participate in any form of abuse *today*, giving or taking, and plan not to participate tomorrow.

You can instruct and serve as a role model for other loved ones and acquaintances today.

Then remember: "There is a Higher Power, and I ain't Him!"

The Serenity Prayer

God grant me the serenity to accept the things I cannot change,
The courage to change the things I can,
And the wisdom to know the difference.

Appendix

INTERVENTION SCRIPT

A minimum of six eyewitnesses of inappropriate behavior will read two statements each using the script below. They will avoid outbursts of anger and any counterattack from the subject of the Intervention. Each will have their written script concise and agreed upon by the entire group.

I speak immediately after_____.

Script

1. _____ (subject's name), I (care, love respect, admire, am committed) to you because _____
_____.

2. I saw or heard you say (time and place specific) _____
_____.

3. When I saw that happen I felt _____
_____ (devastated, concerned, angry, disgusted, betrayed)!

4. I ask you to join in accepting help for my feeling.

Read this second set of four statements while you have the floor.

5. I also care for you because _____
_____.

6. I saw _____ on (incident) _____
_____(time, place).

7. I felt _____
_____.

8. I really want you to seek help for these problems.

Each participant or witness of inappropriate behavior stays with the prepared scripts. "I care for you because... I saw or heard you say... (time and place specific). When I saw that I felt... (scared, concerned, sad, angry). I hope you will join in getting help with my discomfort.

To avoid excessive breaks for him to begin a debate, each person will repeat these four points with a second witnessed incident before the next speaker walks on their words to maintain control of the negotiation. This cuts down on interruptions that the intervenee uses to gain the floor and debate each and every statement. I predict two interruptions of these twelve statements. These are merely typical derailers to divert the negotiation or to take control.

Anger Man

The first will be an anger derailer. The intervenee will say, "I can't believe you have ganged up on me this way. I am really angry at you for doing this!" The group does not want to buy this bait. Assign the person perceived as least likely to interrupt this anger ploy. The preassigned "anger man" will quickly interrupt his statement with this written script: "Of course, we feared this will anger you. If you hate us the rest of our lives, we agreed before we came here to accept that risk. Now, please let (name) finish what she wanted to say to you." This statement may need to be read two or three times if the intervenee interrupts with anger.

Trash Man

The second interruption ploy, typically in this order, will be a "trash" statement. It will go like this: "Wait just a minute! Why are you ganging up on me? What about what she did in 2006? She did a lot worse stuff than I did." The preassigned "trash man" will quickly interrupt this statement. The trash man is the one most calm and least likely to speak up to defend her. If her husband or brother starts defending her, then the group has been derailed and has taken the typical bait. The trash man reads this script: "Sure, you know us all well. We discussed we have issues and agreed to discuss any problem with you at length *later* (meaning later in a family therapy session if arranged). Now, please let the one interrupted finish what she was saying."

DERAIL INTERRUPTIONS

The intervenee may interrupt one of these written statements with an outburst of anger.

_____ (name of assigned person) quickly says, "We care enough for you to risk you even hating us for a long time. Let us ask the one reading their statement to finish speaking.

The intervenee may interrupt another written statement with a counterattack: "What about her problem? Her problem is much worse than mine!"

_____ (name of assigned person) quickly says, "Of course, you know us so well. We all have issues. We promise to discuss any issue with you at length *later.*

Leader

After finally finishing everyone's statements, the leader will try the first request to accept help and say, "This is a tremendous outpouring of love and care for you and of sharing much pain. Your loved ones researched various options for help. We are all joining to ask you to go with _____ (the most acceptable driver) and to agree to receive help there for this pain. Please go there now."

If the answer is "No," leader asks, "In light of all this care and all this pain, what is there that blocks you from accepting help?"

Group will write five probable reasons for rejecting help, agree on response and assign one person to field each objection with an understanding solution to the objection.

SCRIPT

TO PREDICT HIS FIVE EXCUSES

Excuse 1

Leader: "Is there anything that would need to be taken care of so you can go now?"

Intervenee: "I will not go because of _____ (job, money, obligation, kids, privacy issue, etc.)."

Assigned person _____ : "Of course we all knew that is a hurdle. This is why my part was to make _____ (arrangements) to take care of this for you."

Leader: "Well, that is taken care of because these folks care. Let us go now."

Intervenee: "No way, I'm not going!"

Leader: "What else blocks you from going that would need to be taken care of?"

Excuse 2

Intervenee: "I will not go because_____."

Assigned person _____: "Of course we all knew that is a hurdle. This is why my part was to make _____ (arrangements) to take care of this for you. Please go with us now to find help for all our pain."

Excuse 3

Intervenee: "I will not go because _____."

Assigned person _____ : (Write solution.)

Excuse 4

Intervenee: "I will not go because _____."

Assigned person _____ : (Write solution.)

Excuse 5

Intervenee: "I will not go because _____."

Assigned person _____ : (Write solution.)

TRUST-BUILDING SIGN-IN SHEET

You may agree to his "Make Good" trial contingency plan to get help on his own, his way. You may agree if he uses a sign-in sheet to verify his compliance. He may want to use the sign-in sheet to rebuild your trust, in that he is actually working his program by attending some support meeting. Copy or adapt this form.

TRUST-BUILDING SHEET

								Name
								Date / Time
								Group
								Speaker
								Topic
								Signature

CONFLICT IS YOUR FRIEND

PEACE IS NOT THE ABSENSE OF

CONFLICT.

PEACE IS DEALING WITH

CONFLICT

EFFECTIVELY, EFFICENTLY, AND

RESPECTFULLY.

About the Author

AL JAMESON

2005–Present Military and Family Life Consultant, various military installations, from Japan to Turkey

2002–2005 Counselor/Owner, Hope Counseling, Fort Worth, Texas

1998–August 2002 Counselor, Richland Hills Counseling Center, Fort Worth, Texas

1989–August 1998 Counselor, Charter Behavioral Healthcare Systems

Credentials

Master's Degree in Counseling

Licensed Professional Counselor

Licensed Chemical Dependency Counselor

Alcohol and Drug Counselor III, Diplomat

Substance Abuse Professional S.A.P. meeting Department of Transportation Requirements

Texas License LPC Intern Supervisor

American Association of Christian Counselors, Charter Member

Church Deacon and Elder

Past President: Board of Trustees of Independent School District, City Park Board, Trade Association, Civic Organization, and City

Zoning Commission

Active in recovery field since 1973

Dispute resolution mediator and interventionist

Crisis responses and needs assessment

Conference speaker

Active with EAP colleagues

Sent by Charter Hospitals as start-up team leader to Saudi Arabia for six-month assignment

Currently serving under a Department of Defense Contract with Military and Family Members aroud the World